Waves and Vibrations

John Murray
in association with
Inner London Education Authority

APPIL First Edition Project Team
John Bausor (Director)
Leslie Beckett
Allan Covell
David Davies
Martin Hollins

APPIL Revised Edition
Co-ordinated by Martin Hollins
This unit has been revised by Martin Hollins and edited by Allan Covell

Design,typesetting and page layout by Tony Langham
Diagrams by Technical Art Services and John Sangwin

© 1989 Inner London Education Authority

Published by John Murray (Publishers) Ltd,
50 Albemarle Street, London W1X 4BD

APPIL first edition 1979–80
This edition 1989

Printed in Great Britain by J. W. Arrowsmith Ltd, Bristol

British Library Cataloguing in Publication Data

Waves and vibrations
1. Waves   2. Vibration
I. ILEA Physics Project Team   II. Series
531′.1133
531′.32

ISBN 0-7195-4575-7

Contents

How to use APPIL

APPIL is a programme for independent learning. This unit is not a textbook: it is a guide to using texts, experiments and other resources to help you to learn about the topics in your A-level physics syllabus.

There are sections of text in this unit which are to be read as in any other book, but much of the guide is concerned with helping you through other activities designed to produce effective learning when you work independently. For a fuller explanation of the way APPIL is written you should read the *Student's resource book*. What follows is a brief summary.

Objectives

What is to be learnt is stated at the beginning of each topic - a general statement of what you will be doing, and more detailed objectives to be achieved. The objectives are particularly important, because they tell you what you should be able to do when you have finished working through the topic, and so give you extra help in organising your learning. You will probably wish to refer to them when you have finished each topic.

Experiments

E Experiment FM 12
Barton's pendulums

The aim of this experiment is to observe what happens when a system is made to vibrate at some frequency other than its own natural frequency of vibration.

These are a very important part of the course. Each experiment is referred to at the most appropriate time in the text. You should aim to organise your work so that it can be done at that time. Most experiments should not take longer than an hour if the apparatus is available. The experiments are listed at the beginning of each topic, with an estimate of the time required and notes of any other factors to be taken account of in planning. Each experiment contains questions which require written answers. In general, there is no value in copying out the instructions given, but notes on any details which might be useful for revision should be made.

Self-assessment questions

Q 5.19 Self-assessment question

A hi-fi record-player turntable has a mass of 1.28 kg and a radius of gyration about its centre of 25 cm. What is its moment of inertia? What torque will be required to accelerate it up to 33 r.p.m. in 1 second? ■

These test your understanding of the work you have done, and will help you to check your progress. They are not intended to be difficult: you should be able to answer most of them quite easily.

The answers to self-assessment questions are given at the end of the book, but if you look at the answer before you have tried the question you will not be involved in the learning process and your learning may suffer.

■ indicates the end of a question.

Development questions

These are included to involve you in a proof or idea which is being developed in the text. The answer to a development question is usually in the text, but involving yourself in the development helps you to learn: just looking at the answer is not so effective. If the answer is given at the end of the book the question is marked with an asterisk*.

Discussion questions

Q 5.33 Discussion question

Some small toy cars use for propulsion the energy stored in a flywheel; these toys are popularly known as 'friction-powered'. Why? What would be a better name?

How does a yo-yo work?

Can you find any other examples of toys using 'rotatory stores' of energy? How about designing one? ■

These are questions where there is no 'right answer'. Often they cover technical applications, problem-solving and social issues. It is suggested that you do some background research and reading - or just thinking, to answer these.

Study questions

For these you will need to use resources apart from this unit: for example, textbooks or experimental results. For all questions, general references are given to basic books at the start of each topic. It is not expected that you will be able to consult all the references given but you should always use more than one when possible.

This type of question usually requires longer answers than the others. These answers, in many cases, form a basis for your notes for the final examination and are therefore very important. Full answers are not usually given in this guide, though hints and partial answers are sometimes given. These questions are marked with an asterisk. Your answers to study questions should be handed in regularly for marking.

Questions on objectives

These are groups of questions which come at the end of each topic and are related to the objectives at the beginning of each topic. Answering these will help you to tell whether you have achieved the objectives. The answers are given in the *Student's resource book*.

End-of-unit test

This is to enable your teacher to check the value of the course to you. You will be asked to do this test when you have completed the unit, and will be given details at the appropriate time.

Examination questions

Questions in the test, and some of the other questions, are taken from past papers. Your teacher will probably set some more of these during the course, for revision purposes.

Audio-visual aids /Computer programs

C Computer program
Simple harmonic motion

This program enables you to explore simple harmonic motion and its relationship with uniform circular motion.

Audio - visual aids and computer programs are recommended in some topics. You should ask your teacher if these are available.

Background reading

Background reading

For an exciting account of the work of Galileo and Newton, read Koestler, A. *The sleepwalkers.*

This refers to books which are useful for a more detailed study of certain topics. They are also often interesting to read in their own right, and sometimes put the physics of the syllabus in its historical, social or technological context.

References

References are made where appropriate to textbooks. A list of the abbreviations used can be found at the end of this unit.

Comprehension

C Comprehension FM 2
Building the wind-up tube train

This is an article on the use of flywheels in the New York underground system.

These extracts from recent scientific and technological articles have a similar aim. They are followed by questions designed to check your understanding. They will be found in Part 4 of the *Student's resource book.*

Extension

EXTENSION

Q 2.30 Study question

(a) Why is a violin box shaped the way it is? (b) How can a violinist change the quality of note produced by this instrument? (c) In what other shapes are sound boxes made? Suggest how they affect the sound produced.■

These boxed sections are included to provide:

(a) additional material of general interest and importance, or
(b) more detailed treatment of topics for more able students.

Sections marked ● are not required for some syllabuses and may provide additional useful extension material. Your teacher will advise you of the particular requirements of your syllabus.

Organising your time

In this programme of work there is a variety of activities. Some of them, like experiments, need a laboratory, and you may also need to use the library. You must, therefore, organise your time so that you can make the best use of the resources available.

When you start a topic, look through it and see what activities are included, then allocate each activity a time on your work schedule. Make sure, for example, that you do the experiments when you are timetabled in a laboratory. Follow the sequence in this guide if you can, but this may not always be possible.

The recommended time for completion of the work in each topic is given at the beginning of each topic. This assumes that you spend 8-10 hours each week on physics, divided between class time, private study and home study. It is important to try to complete the unit in a set time. You should ask your teacher for a **progress monitor**. It will help you to plan your time.

Introduction to the unit

This unit introduces the powerful model of wave behaviour and develops its use in many areas of physics.

This unit is one of the recommended starting points for the course, so there is a preliminary section, the *starting block*. This reviews some of your earlier physics studies which are relevant to this unit, and includes a preliminary test and advice on how to fill any gaps in your knowledge.

Topic 1 develops the idea of a wave model by studying the properties of mechanical waves, in springs and on the surface of water.

Topic 2 is a study of sound which shows clearly all the classical wave properties, including the Doppler effect.

Topic 3 introduces the idea that light is a wave, but is mainly concerned with a geometric approach, using rays to study reflection, refraction and the design of optical instruments.

Topic 4 looks in detail at the wave nature of the whole electromagnetic spectrum, how the various types of radiation are produced and detected, and their various uses.

Topic 5 is mainly about the superposition of light through interference and diffraction, and the importance of these effects in image formation and the analysis of spectra.

Recommended study times

You should spend 8-10 weeks on this unit as follows:-

Topic 1   2 weeks
Topic 2   2-2.5 weeks
Topic 3   1.5-2 weeks
Topic 4   0.5-1 week
Topic 5   1.5-2 weeks

Starting block

It is assumed that you have studied physics before, so the unit will build on and extend your present knowledge. Since you may have forgotten some of the things you learnt, or there may be a few things you are not sure about, this section is designed to help you to revise, re-learn or learn what you need to know to make the best use of this unit.

Start by reading the pre-requisite objectives: these are the things you need to be able to do before you begin work on the main part of the unit.

Work through the preliminary test, which consists of questions based on the pre-requisite objectives. Go quickly through all parts of the test without reference to books or to any other person.

The aim of the test is to enable you to check what you know now so that you can find and fill up any gaps in your own knowledge.

Mark your own test when you have finished, following the marking instructions. Then read the directions for using your test result, and do any follow-up work recommended.

When you have done this, you will be able to start Topic 1 with confidence, knowing that you are ready to tackle new work.

Pre-requisite objectives

Before starting this unit you should be able to:

1 Use the following scientific terms correctly: displacement, amplitude, frequency, wavelength, medium, wave, wave speed, period.

2 Interpret a graph of particle displacement plotted against time.

3 Use the following scientific terms correctly: reflection, refraction, real image, virtual image, angle of incidence, angle of reflection, normal, angle of refraction.

4 Recall the relationship between angle of incidence and angle of reflection when light is reflected from a smooth surface.

5 Recall the type and nature of the image formed by a plane mirror.

6 Sketch the paths of rays of light from an object, reflected by a plane mirror to the eye, showing how the image is located.

7 Recall the effect on a ray of light reflected from a plane mirror when the mirror is rotated about an axis perpendicular to the plane containing incident ray, normal and reflected ray.

8 State the meaning of refraction, and sketch the path of rays of light which pass from one medium to another (for example, from air to glass).

9 Recall the effects of a prism on a narrow beam of white light.

10 Use the following scientific terms correctly: converging rays, diverging rays, converging (convex) lens, diverging (concave) lens, focal length, erect image, inverted image, magnification, concave mirror, convex mirror.

11 Explain the difference between a real image and virtual image.

12 Determine, by graphical construction, the positions, sizes and natures of the images formed by a concave mirror for different positions of the object.

13 Determine, by graphical construction, the positions, sizes and natures of the images formed by a converging lens for different positions of the object.

Preliminary test

There are three types of question in this test, coded as follows:
MC Multiple choice. Select the single best answer.
MR Multiple response. Select all the correct answers.
NUM Numerical answer (including diagrams). Work out the answer and write it down, including the unit where appropriate.

Part A Wave terms

Questions 1-3 *MC*

Which of the quantities (A-E) below is described in each of the questions 1-3?

A frequency
B wavelength
C period
D wave speed
E amplitude

1 The maximum displacement of a particle from its rest position.

2 The number of complete vibrations made in 1 second.

3 The distance between two adjacent crests of a wave.

Questions 4-6 *MC*

Figure P1 shows the waveforms of five notes (A-E), displayed one after the other on a cathode ray oscilloscope, without adjusting its controls.

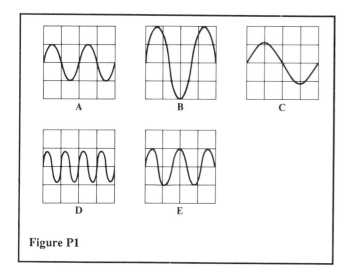

Figure P1

4 Which note has the largest amplitude?

5 Which note has the lowest frequency?

6 Which note has the highest frequency?

Questions 7 and 8 *MR*

The displacement-time graph, figure P2, shows how the displacement of a particle at a particular distance from a source of vibration varies with time. Which of the distances marked (A-G) are equal to the quantities in questions 7 and 8?

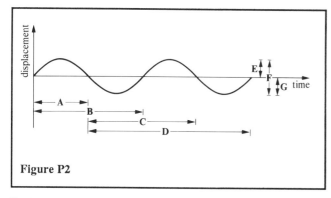

Figure P2

7 The period of the vibration.

8 The amplitude of the vibration.

Part B Reflection and refraction

9 *MC* Which of the following (A-D) shows the image of a letter P placed in front of a plane mirror?

A P
B ꟼ
C q
D d

10 *NUM* A student faces a plane mirror, which is 5 metres in front of her. How far must she move so that she is 4 metres nearer to her image?

11 *NUM* A ray of light strikes a plane mirror so that the reflected ray makes an angle of 30° with the incident ray. The mirror is turned through an angle of 20°, first clockwise then anticlockwise, about an axis at right angles to the plane of the rays. For each case, what is the angle between the incident ray and the new reflected ray?

12 *NUM* An object O is placed between two plane mirrors which are arranged at right angles to each other. The object is 2 cm from one mirror and 3 cm from the other. Sketch a diagram showing the positions of the images that are produced.

13 *MC* Which of the diagrams (A-D) in figure P3 shows correctly the path of a ray of light passing through a glass block?

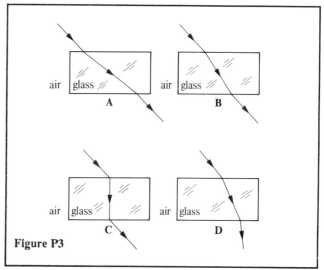

Figure P3

14 *MC* When white light is passed through a prism, which of the following colours is refracted through the smallest angle?

A yellow
B red
C green
D blue

Part C Mirrors and lenses

Questions 15-19 *MC*

From the descriptions of optical images (A-E) below, choose the correct description for the image formed in each of the cases specified in questions 15-19.

A real and diminished
B real and enlarged
C virtual and diminished
D virtual and the same size as the object
E virtual and enlarged

15 A plane mirror.

16 A convex driving mirror.

17 A camera lens used to photograph a distant object.

18 A concave mirror used as a shaving mirror.

19 A converging lens used as a magnifying glass.

20 *MC* An object is placed between a concave mirror and its principal focus. Which of the statements (A-E) correctly describes the image which is formed?

A virtual, erect and diminished
B virtual, erect and enlarged
C real, inverted and diminished
D real, inverted and the same size as the object
E real, inverted and enlarged

Questions 21-24 *NUM*

An object 3.0 cm tall is placed 30.0 cm from a concave mirror of focal length 10.0 cm so that it is perpendicular to, and has one end on, the axis of the mirror. Determine, by graphical construction, the answers to questions 21-24.

21 What is the distance of the image from the mirror?

22 What is the height of the image?

23 Is the image erect or inverted?

24 Is the image real or virtual?

Questions 25-27 *MC*

Figure P4 shows a converging lens with five possible *object* positions (A-E) marked on the axis. Select from these the correct object position for each of the types of image described in questions 25-27.

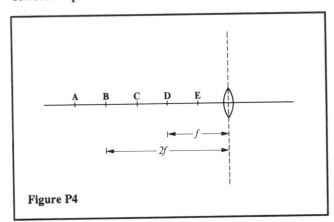

Figure P4

25 Virtual and erect.

26 Real and diminished.

27 Real and enlarged.

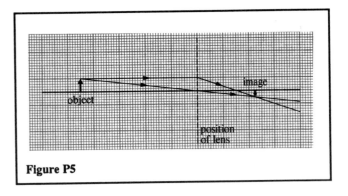

Figure P5

Questions 28-32 *NUM*

Figure P5 is a ray diagram (drawn to scale) illustrating the formation of the image of an object, 1.0 cm tall, placed 9.0 cm away from the lens.

28 What type of lens is used?

29 What is the focal length of the lens?

30 How far is the image from the lens?

31 Is the image real or virtual?

32 What is the magnification of the image?

Questions 33-36 *NUM*

An object 4.0 cm tall is placed 6.0 cm from a converging (convex) lens of focal length 18.0 cm. The object is perpendicular to, and has one end on, the axis of the lens. Determine, by graphical construction, the answers to questions 33-36.

33 What is the distance of the image from the lens?

34 What is the height of the image?

35 Is the image erect or inverted?

36 Is the image real or virtual?

Marking

Compare your answers with those given opposite, and give yourself one mark for each fully correct answer. To be fully correct, only the right answer should be given for multiple choice questions, all the right answers and no wrong ones for multiple response questions, and the unit as well as the number for numerical questions. Add up your marks for each part of the test separately.

Answers

Part A *8 marks*

1 E
2 A
3 B
4 B
5 C
6 D
7 B,C
8 E,G

Part B *6 marks*

9 C
10 2 metre
11 70°, 10° (figure P6)

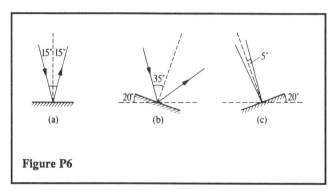

Figure P6

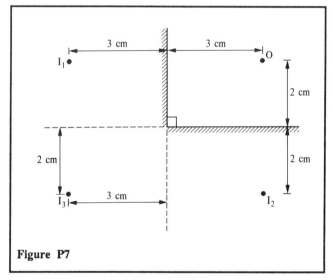

Figure P7

12 Figure P7 shows the positions of all three images.
13 B
14 B

Part C *22 marks*

15 D
16 C
17 A
18 E
19 E
20 B
21 15.0 cm (figure P8)
22 1.5 cm
23 Inverted
24 Real

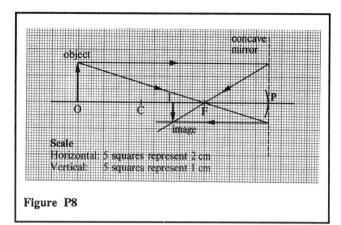

Figure P8

25 E
26 A
27 C
28 A converging (convex) lens
29 3.0 cm
30 4.5 cm
31 Real
32 0.5
33 9.0 cm (figure P9)
34 6.0 cm
35 Erect
36 Virtual

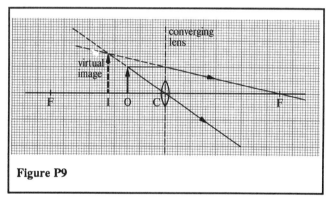

Figure P9

Using the test results

The pre-requisite objectives were tested as follows.

Objectives 1 and 2	Part A
Objectives 3,4,5,6,7,8 and 9	Part B
Objectives 10,11,12 and 13	Part C

Your marks in the preliminary test indicate whether you need to do some follow-up work before starting topics 1 and 3. The flow chart (figure P10) will direct you along your own personal route through any necessary revision sections in the following *Revision block*.

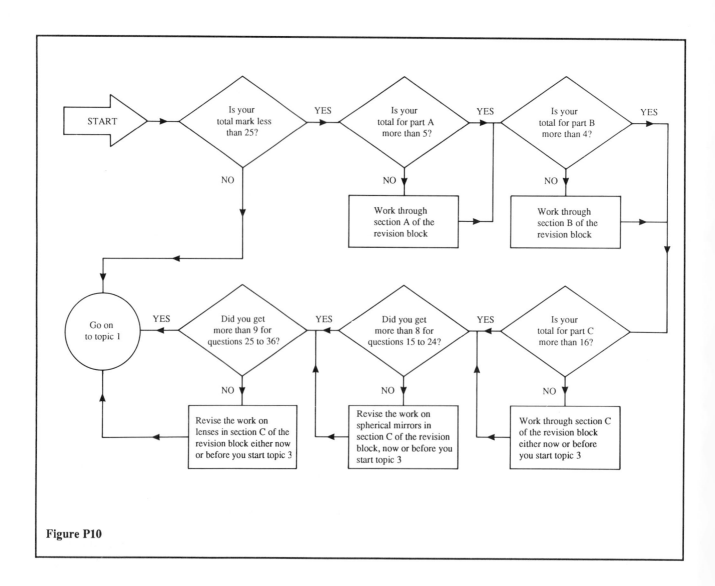

Figure P10

Revision block

References to relevant chapters of GCSE textbooks are given in each section. Use these references in answering the questions and in checking that you understand the relevant pre-requisite objectives. Answers are given in the 'Answers' section for questions marked*.

A Wave terms

References

Avison   Chapter 20
Duncan GCSE   Chapter 13
Duncan SIP   Unit 16.2

Use the references listed above in answering the following questions.

Q R 1 Define wavelength, frequency and wave speed of a wave. ■

Q R 2 Figure P11 shows how the displacement of a particle at a certain distance from the source of vibration varies with time. Copy this graph, and mark the amplitude a of the wave and period T of the vibration. ■

Refer back to pre-requisite objectives 1 and 2 to confirm that you have now achieved these objectives.

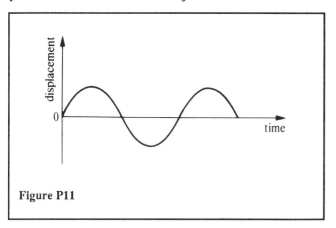

Figure P11

B Reflection and refraction

References

Avison   Chapters 1 and 2
Duncan GCSE   Chapters 1-3 and 5
Duncan SIP   Unit 13.5, 14.1

Use the references listed above in answering the following questions.

Q R 3 State the laws of reflection of light, and outline how you would test them experimentally. ■

Q R 4 Show that the image of a real object in a plane mirror is as far behind the mirror as the object is in front. Outline how you would test this experimentally. What is meant by the statement that this image is virtual? ■

Q R 5 Figure P12 shows a point object O in front of two vertical plane mirrors which are placed at right angles to each other.
Copy this diagram and complete the paths of two rays from O to show how the images I_1 and I_2 are formed. Mark on your diagram the position of a third image I_3. ■

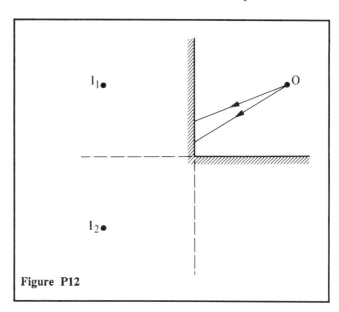

Figure P12

Q R 6 State *four* properties of the image of a real object formed by a plane mirror. ■

Q R 7 Show that a ray of light reflected from a plane mirror rotates through an angle of 2θ when the mirror rotates through an angle of θ. ■

Q R 8 Explain, with the aid of a diagram, what is meant by refraction. Show on your diagram the incident ray, the refracted ray and the normal, and mark the angle of incidence and the angle of refraction. ■

***Q R 9** Figure P13 shows the path of a ray of light entering a block of glass.

(a) What is the angle of incidence on the surface AB?
(b) What is the angle of refraction at this surface? ■

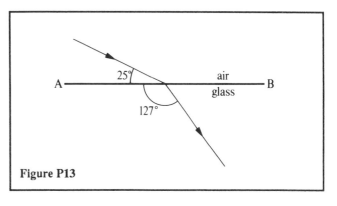

Figure P13

Q R 10 Explain, with the aid of a diagram, what happens when a narrow beam of white light passes through a triangular glass prism. ■

Refer back to pre-requisite objectives 3, 4, 5, 6, 7, 8 and 9 to confirm that you have now achieved these objectives.

C Mirrors and lenses

References

Avison   Chapters 1 and 3
Duncan GCSE   Chapters 3, 4 and 7
Duncan SIP   Unit 13.6-13.9 and 14.5-14.7

Use the references listed above in answering the following questions.

Q R 11 Explain the difference between a real image and a virtual image.■

Q R 12 Show on a ray diagram the centre of curvature C, pole P and principal focus F of a concave mirror.■

Q R 13 Draw ray diagrams to show how, for a real object, a concave mirror forms

(a) an enlarged real image,
(b) a virtual image.■

Q R 14 Copy and complete the following table, to summarise the positions and natures of the images formed by a concave mirror for different positions of the object.

Position of object	Position of image	Nature of image
At infinity	at F	real, inverted, diminished.
Between infinity and C		
At C		
Between C and F		
At F		
Between F and P		

■

*Q R 15 An object is placed in front of a concave mirror of focal length 15.0 cm so that it is at right angles to, and has one end resting on, the axis of the mirror. It forms an erect image which is 30.0 cm from the mirror and 6.0 cm high. Find, by graphical construction, the position and height of the object.■

Q R 16 Explain, with the aid of a ray diagram, the terms principal focus F, optical centre C and focal length f as applied to converging lens.■

Q R 17 Draw ray diagrams to show how, for a real object, a converging lens forms
(a) a real diminished image,
(b) a virtual image.■

Q R 18 Copy and complete the following table, to summarise the positions and natures of the images formed by a converging lens for different positions of a real object (figure P14).

Position of object	Position of image	Nature of image
At infinity	at F_2	real, inverted, diminished.
Between infinity and P		
At P		
Between P and F_1		
At F_1		
Between C and F_1		

*Q R 19 An object 2.0 cm tall is placed 8.0 cm from a converging lens so that it is at right angles to, and has one end on, the axis of the lens. The object forms a real image 16.0 cm from the lens. Find, by graphical construction,

(a) the focal length of the lens,
(b) the position of the object for which a virtual image is formed equal in size to the former real image.■

Refer back to the pre-requisite objects 10, 11, 12 and 13 to confirm that you have now achieved these objectives.

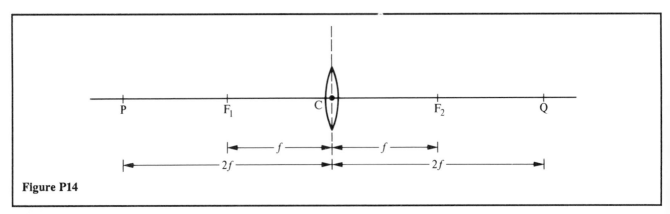

Figure P14

TOPIC 1

Wave models

Summary

The wave model is an important way of describing parts of the working of the universe. Here we extend a study of tangible waves (those in springs and on the surface of water) to those we cannot see or touch. The photograph of ripples shows one key feature of wave behaviour. What is it?

Objectives

When you have completed the work in this topic you should be able to:

1   Use the following scientific terms correctly: phase angle, phase difference, wave pulse, diffraction, wave train, interference, superposition, mechanical wave, electromagnetic wave, progressive wave, sinusoidal wave.

2   Define the following terms: wavelength, wavefront, amplitude, period, frequency, angular frequency, dispersion.

3   Distinguish between longitudinal and transverse waves, and give examples of each.

4   Derive, recall and use the relationship between wave speed, frequency, and wavelength.

$$c = f\lambda$$

5   Recall examples of reflection of waves, with and without phase change.

6   Predict the forms of the reflected wavefronts when plane or circular waves are reflected from straight or curved barriers.

7   Give qualitative explanations of the refraction and diffraction of waves, with suitable examples.

8   State the principle of superposition.

9   Explain qualitatively, using diagrams, how an interference pattern is produced by superposition of waves from two point sources of the same frequency, and give examples of this phenomenon.

10   Describe, with diagrams and/or graphs, the relationship for a progressive wave between
(a) displacement and time, for a particular point in a medium,
(b) displacement and distance, at a particular instant.

11   Explain, with the aid of models such as springs and coupled dynamics trolleys, the factors affecting the speed of transverse waves in strings and wires.

12   Solve problems involving the equation for the speed of transverse waves along a string or wire.

$$c = \sqrt{\frac{T}{\mu}}$$

Experiments

WV 1 Observing wave pulses   (0.75 hour)
WV 2 Waves in a ripple tank   (1 hour)
WV 3 Investigating pulse speed   (0.75 hour)

References

Akrill	Chapter 23
Bolton	Chapter 7
Duncan	Chapter 8
Muncaster	Chapters 23 and 31
Nelkon	Chapter 17
Whelan	Chapters 12 and 14

1.1 Mechanical wave models

Waves are very common, varied and important phenomena. Animals, including humans, explore their environment through sound and light waves. We communicate by waves; indeed, it is difficult to think of any method of communication, ancient or modern, which does not use waves. Waves also provide the most important means of transferring energy, including the energy of the sun, which is so vital to our needs on earth. When a wave transfers energy and momentum from the wave source to places around it, we describe it as a **progressive** or **travelling** wave.

In science, models are used to help in explaining observations and predicting effects. A model may be a diagram, a constructed object, a physical situation, or even a mathematical equation. We use models in everyday life. A London underground map is a good model of the underground system. It is certainly not an exact replica of the rail system. For one thing, it is not drawn to scale and the actual lines and trains are not red, brown, yellow or blue as the map suggests. Nevertheless, it is a good model because it can *explain* why if we travel on a certain line we will pass through King's Cross and it can *predict* that if we get on a particular train we can end up in the Essex marshes!

No one can see a *wave* of light, and it is not easy to observe the effects produced when sound travels through air. A wave model helps us to visualise and explain what is happening when waves like light, sound, X-rays, and so on, are produced and transmitted. The wave model will be developed by observing waves in springs, and on the surface of water. These are **mechanical waves**, which are produced when some part of an elastic medium is displaced from its equilibrium position, for example, when a stone is dropped on to a water surface or a loudspeaker makes particles of air vibrate.

Q 1.1 Development question*

Figure 1.1 shows the cross-section of a water surface just after a small stone has been dropped on to it.
(a) How does this diagram support the fact that water is almost incompressible?
(b) What forces act to move particles in the water which are some distance from the stone?
(c) Sketch a section through the water surface a moment after that shown in figure 1.1, marking the reference lines O, X and Y.
(d) What happens to the original kinetic energy of the stone?
(e) Suggest a reason why the water does not immediately become calm again.■

Note. Answers to development questions are sometimes given at the back of the book, as in this case, but are often incorporated in the question or in the following text.

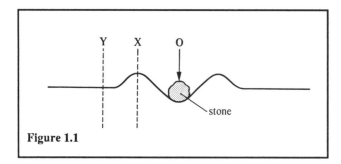

Figure 1.1

Elastic is the term used to describe 'springiness' (the capacity of a substance to return to its original shape and size after being deformed). When a particle in an elastic medium is displaced from its equilibrium position, forces act on the particle which will tend to restore it to its original position. Because the particle has inertia (resistance to change in motion), it will overshoot the equilibrium position and oscillate. All the particles in the medium are interconnected by forces, and the displacement of one particle will change the forces acting on other particles close to it. These particles will then be displaced. This interaction between the particles causes a disturbance to spread through the medium and produces a transfer of energy. The moving disturbance is a wave, and the energy transfer can be detected (for example, by a floating cork for water waves or a microphone for sound waves).

Therefore, a mechanical wave transmits mechanical energy through a material medium which has inertia and elasticity.

Electromagnetic waves form a second group of waves. These include light, radio and X-rays. You will study evidence that light has wave properties in topic 3 and the nature of electromagnetic waves in topic 4. However, many of the properties of these complex three-dimensional waves can be understood by studying a simple kind of wave - a one-dimensional wave pulse in a long spring or rope.

1.2 Wave pulses

When you slam the door of a room, the air in the doorway is compressed rapidly. This single compression travels as a disturbance across the room and gives a sudden push to the curtains. The air particles have not travelled across the room in that time, but energy has. This short-duration wave is called a **pulse.**

Q 1.2 Self-assessment question

(a) In an obstacle race a competitor has to crawl under a tarpaulin sheet, causing a bump to travel along the sheet. Is this moving disturbance a progressive wave pulse? Explain.
(b) If you look down on a line of cars queuing at traffic lights, you will observe a 'pulse of starting' move along the line of cars when the traffic light changes to green. Which way does the 'pulse of starting' travel, and what does its speed depend on?■

A distinction must always be made between the movement of the particles of the medium and the movement of the wave pulse through the medium.

E Experiment WV 1
Observing wave pulses

Different types of wave pulse can be observed moving along a stretched spring or rubber tube and the pulse speeds can be estimated.

Q 1.3 Self-assessment question

Figure 1.2 shows a series of pictures taken at regular intervals illustrating how a pulse of compressed coils moves along a slinky spring.

(a) Which way does the 10th coil from the left move between instant 2 and instant 4?
(b) Is this coil moving at instant 5? If so, in which direction?
(c) Is it possible to say in which direction this coil is moving at instant 7? Explain.■

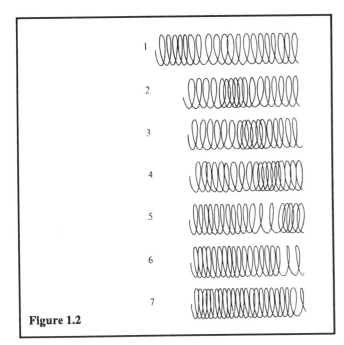

Figure 1.2

The kind of pulse shown in figure 1.2 is a **longitudinal** pulse, which can travel only through a medium which can be compressed. **Transverse** pulses can only travel through a medium in which the particles can be displaced across the direction in which the pulse travels, and come back.

Twisting the end of a slinky clockwise and then anti-clockwise will produce **torsional** waves, in which particles of the spring have an angular displacement in a plane perpendicular to the direction in which the wave pulse travels. If a violin bow produces torsional waves in a string, a high-pitched squeal is produced. This explains why inexperienced violinists quickly lose their audiences!

Q 1.4 Self-assessment question

What kinds of mechanical waves can be transmitted in

(a) a gas,
(b) a solid? ■

Representing waves graphically

In physics we must be able to view the same event in more than one way. Sometimes we view the 'individual trees', sometimes the 'whole wood'. In studying mechanical waves we must consider how a wave travels through a medium (a view of the 'whole wood') and also what happens to individual particles of the medium (a view of each 'tree'). Thus, two kinds of graph are used to represent mechanical waves (and other wave motion).

1 Displacement-distance graphs, showing the position (displacement) of every point along the medium at a particular moment of time t (displacement y against distance x, for a fixed value of t).

2 Displacement-time graphs, showing what happens to the displacement of a particular point as the time changes (displacement y against t, for a fixed value of x).

Q 1.5 Self-assessment question

Which type of graph is displayed on a cathode ray oscilloscope showing the waveform of a sound wave picked up by a microphone? ■

Q 1.6 Development question*

Figure 1.3a shows the shape of a pulse travelling from left to right along a rope.

(a)   Sketch a graph of displacement along the rope at a particular instant (y against x).
(b)   Sketch a graph showing how the displacement of P changes as this pulse passes (y against t). Indicate how the y against t graph would change if the wave speed were to be doubled, for this same shape of pulse.
(c)   Sketch a graph of y against t for point P if the wave pulse has the same shape but travels with speed c in the opposite direction (figure 1.3b). ■

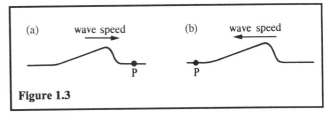

Figure 1.3

Q 1.7 Self-assessment question

The diagram (figure 1.4) shows a transverse wave pulse in a string travelling at 4 m s⁻¹ in the direction of the arrow.
(a) Draw a graph to show precisely how the displacement of P from its equilibrium position varies with time over an interval of 0.3 s from the instant shown in the figure.
(b) How could you find the transverse velocity of P at any instant? ■

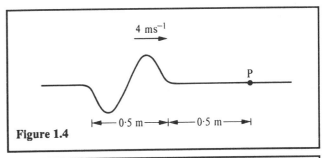

Figure 1.4

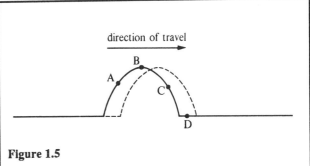

Figure 1.5

Information about the motion of different points in the medium can also be obtained by analysing the position of the pulse at two close successive instants of time. Figure 1.5 shows two such positions of a transverse wave pulse in a rope, in which the particles only move at right angles to the direction of the moving pulse.

Q 1.8 Self-assessment question

(a) Sketch the diagram (figure 1.5) and mark the displacement of points A, B, C and D during the time interval.
(b) Which points are moving in the same direction?
(c) Which of these points moves with (i) greatest,
(ii) least average speed during the interval?
(d) At what point in the pulse is the rope momentarily at rest? ■

Superposition of wave pulses

What happens when waves meet? Your observations of wave pulses will have revealed a surprising thing. Waves pass through each other and the waves emerge unaffected by this meeting. We can hear music from a radio even though many other sound waves are crossing the line between the radio and our ear. Communication would be impossible if waves bumped into each other as material particles do.

When more than one wave affects the same point in a medium, the waves are said to be **superposed**. The effect is summarised in the **principle of superposition**.

Q 1.9 Study question

Write a precise statement of the principle of superposition. Illustrate the principle with a graphical example, and indicate why the word 'vector' is important in the statement. Does the principle apply only to wave pulses? What types of wave does it apply to? When does it break down? ■

Using references in answering a study question

References are given at the beginning of each chapter. Some are to general physics textbooks, others are to books on more specific topics. In all the references given you will find parts which are not relevant to a particular question. There are two ways of dealing with this effectively.

1 Use the *index*. Read through the question and choose the *key words* from it, and look for index references to these. In question 1.9, for example, a key word is 'superposition'. Reading more than one explanation will help your understanding.

2 Use *sub-headings* to find relevant sections of the chapters. Skim through these sections and make brief notes of the points you want to include in your answer.

For more help on how to make notes, consult the APPIL *Student's resource book* and read the relevant chapter in *Use your head* by Tony Buzan.

Q 1.10 Self-assessment question

Figure 1.6 shows two equal and opposite pulses approaching each other on a long string. The pulses are 0.8 m long, each

is travelling at 2 m s⁻¹, and their leading edges are 0.4 m apart at the instant shown.
(a) Sketch diagrams to show the shape of the string at times 0.1 s, 0.2 s, 0.3 s, 0.4 s and 0.5 s later than the instant shown.
(b) How does point O move during this period?
(c) Each wave pulse carries energy. What has happened to that energy at $t = 0.3$ s? ■

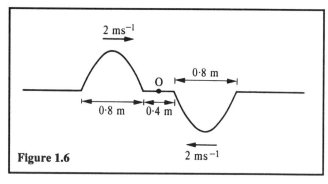

Figure 1.6

Q 1.11 Self-assessment question

Figure 1.7 shows a sequence of photographs taken as two equal symmetrical pulses approach each other along a spring. The spring appears blurred in places, due to its movement during an exposure.

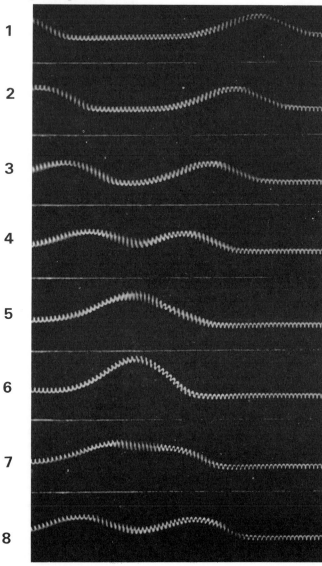

Figure 1.7

(a) Use the principle of superposition to explain the directions of motion of the blurred sections of spring in photographs 5 and 7 (figure 1.7).

(b) Explain why there is an instant (photograph 6, figure 1.7) when no part of the spring is moving.

(c) How can you tell from the photographs that the sequence of events goes from top to bottom, and not from bottom to top? ∎

Pulses at a boundary

Q 1.12 Self-assessment question

When a transverse pulse on a spring reaches a rigid support, the reflected pulse is upside down (figure 1.8a).
In terms of the forces on the support and on the spring, explain why this happens. ∎

When a pulse reaches the free end of a spring the only way it can travel is backwards, as a reflected pulse. Since there is no external force acting on the spring, there is no change in the total momentum when the pulse is reflected, so an upright pulse is reflected as an upright pulse (figure 1.8b).

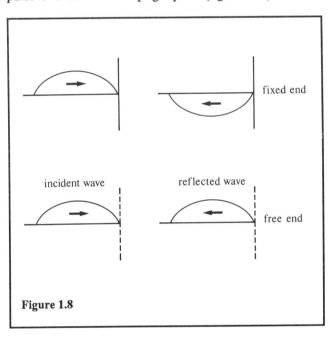

Figure 1.8

Q 1.13 Self-assessment question

Explain why one of the reflected pulses in figure 1.8 is said to be in phase, the other 180° or π rad out of phase. ∎

When a pulse meets a boundary between two media (for example, a light spring and a heavy spring), the energy is partly transmitted through the boundary and partly reflected back. Figure 1.9 shows a pulse travelling from a light spring to a heavy spring. Notice that the reflected pulse is upside down, like that from a rigid support, but some energy is transmitted to the heavy spring.

What happens when a compression wave pulse is reflected? We cannot now talk of upside-down and right-side-up reflection. However, a compression pulse arriving at a fixed or a free end may produce a reflected compression or a reflected rarefaction.

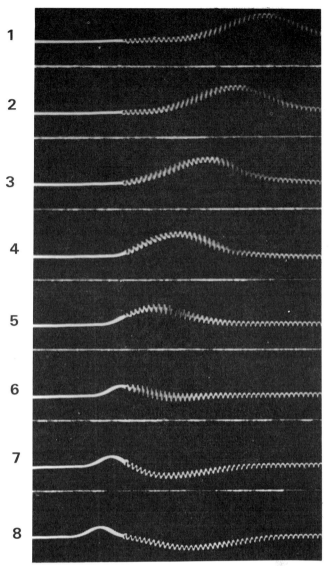

Figure 1.9

Q 1.14 Study question

Make notes or draw sketches to show the difference between the reflection of a compression pulse at a fixed and at a free end of a slinky. ∎

This study of pulses in springs may seem very remote from the study of more important waves like light and sound. However, you will find that this study of pulses provides important clues to understanding topics to be studied later. For example, in topic 2 you will study how sound waves can be reflected from both closed and open ends of pipes and how the reflection of light travelling from air to glass is not quite the same as the reflection when light is travelling from glass to air. A single travelling wave pulse which can propagate energy in one dimension only (along the spring) is a good model to study at the beginning.

1.3 Periodic waves

A periodic change is one in which the pattern of change repeats itself at regular intervals: the water level at London Bridge undergoes a periodic change; the motion of a bird's wing in flight is periodic; your pulse is periodic.

The periodic motion of a body can produce a periodic mechanical wave in the surrounding medium. For example, a dipper vibrating in a ripple tank produces a periodic wave train of ripples. A vibrating loudspeaker produces a sound wave: a periodic travelling longitudinal wave.

Q 1.15 Study question

Define the period and frequency of a periodic change. What is the relationship between period and frequency? In what units is frequency measured? ∎

There are many kinds of periodic motion. One of the simplest and most common is called simple harmonic motion (s.h.m.). The displacement of an object vibrating with s.h.m. varies with time according to a sinusoidal curve (figure 1.10a). The wave train produced by such a source has a sinusoidal profile, so the graph of displacement y against distance x, along the direction of propagation, is as shown in figure 1.10b. Graphs similar to figure 1.10a can be used to describe the variation of the displacement of other points in the vibrating medium with time.

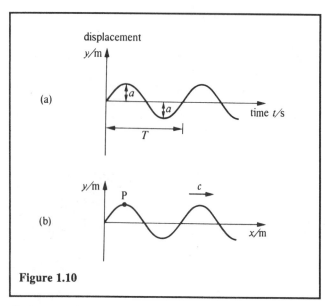

Figure 1.10

Q 1.16 Self-assessment question

(a) Sketch a graph of y against t for a particle in the vibrating medium which is at P when $t = 0$ (figure 1.10b). Label the amplitude a and the period T on your graph.
(b) How can you find the velocity of the vibrating particle at any instant from the graph?
(c) When is the velocity of the particle (i) maximum, and (ii) zero?
(d) Do particles with the same displacement always have the same velocity? ∎

Q 1.17 Development question*

Figure 1.11 shows two instantaneous positions of a periodic wave travelling along a string whose left hand end is attached to a vertically moving vibrator.
(a) Which pairs of points marked on the string have, at the instant shown, (i) the same displacement but velocities in opposite directions, (ii) equal and opposite displacements but the same velocity, (iii) the same displacement and velocity?
(b) In what way is the motion of point B similar to the motion of point A, and in what way is it different?

(c) Which points are vibrating 'in step' ? (Such vibrations are described as **in phase**).
(d) How far will the waveform travel to the right as the vibrator makes one complete vibration? Explain your answer.
(e) If the distance AE along the wave is 1.2 m, and the vibrator makes a complete vibration in 0.5 s, what is the speed at which the wave crests are travelling? ∎

In the last question you considered the motion of five particular points on the string which had displacements of the same size. Now think about the motion of any point on the string.

Q 1.18 Self-assessment question

(a) What quantities are the same for the vibrations of any two points along the string (assuming no energy is lost as the wave travels along the string)?
(b) Explain the terms **in phase** and **phase lag** by referring to vibrating points on the string in figure 1.11.
(c) 'The distance between two consecutive points which are in phase is constant, for a wave of fixed speed and frequency'. Explain and justify this statement, referring to figure 1.11. ∎

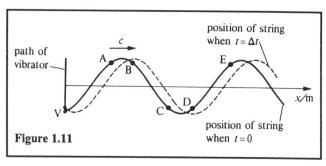

Figure 1.11

Q 1.19 Self-assessment question

(a) Show that
wave speed = frequency x wavelength

$$c = f\lambda$$

(b) What changes would you observe in a ripple tank if you reduced the frequency of the vibrating dipper?
(c) The speed of radio waves is 3×10^8 m s^{-1}. What is the frequency of the waves broadcasting Radio 4 on 1500 m? ∎

Q 1.20 Self-assessment question

Figure 1.12 is a graph of y against x for a wave travelling with speed c. Draw the corresponding y against t graph for point P, marking the value of t for each instant when $y = 0$. Express the values of t in terms of λ and c. ∎

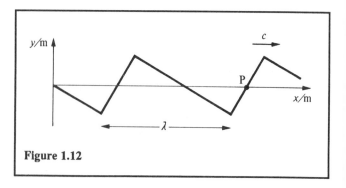

Figure 1.12

1.4 Waves in two dimensions

So far in this topic the properties of waves have been studied using a one-dimensional wave model - a wave on a string. Now we can extend our study by observing what happens in a plane in two-dimensional space. We can do this by looking at two-dimensional waves (e.g. ripples on a water surface) and also by considering the effects produced in a particular plane by three-dimensional waves.

Wavefronts

A wavefront is a surface containing all points for which the disturbance has the same phase. We can also think of a wavefront as the surface containing all points in the moving wave which left the source at the same instant. For one-dimensional waves the wavefront is a moving point and for two-dimensional waves the wavefront is a line. A circular crest radiating from a point disturbance of a water surface is a wavefront; so also is a radiating trough, or any other line on the surface which satisfies the definition above. When representing periodic waves we often draw a series of wavefronts which differ in phase by 2π rad (that is, at separations of one wavelength).

Wavefronts move outwards from the source, and lines drawn perpendicular to the wavefront indicate the direction in which energy is radiating. In the study of light we refer to these lines as **rays**, but the term can be applied to all kinds of radiating energy waves.

Q 1.21 Self-assessment question

(a) What kind of wavefront is produced by a point source if the wave speed is the same for all directions in the medium?
(b) How would you draw this wavefront in a plane passing through the point source?
(c) If plane wavefronts arrive at a long narrow slit, what shape are the emerging wavefronts?
(d) How would you draw these wavefronts in a plane perpendicular to the length of the slit? ■

E Experiment WV 2
Waves in a ripple tank

You will use this equipment to generate wave pulses and continuous waves on a water surface. From your observations you can draw some conclusions about wave behaviour.

Reflection of waves

Observations in the ripple tank show how water waves obey the laws of reflection. They can be reflected so that the wave energy is focused to a point, or so that the waves appear to come from a 'virtual image point'. You may have already studied these effects by observing ray streaks (streaks of light perpendicular to the wavefront); in the ripple tank you observe the wavefronts themselves. So there are two different ways of describing and visualising the same effects.

Q 1.22 Self-assessment question

In figure 1.13, a straight wave pulse approaches a right-angled reflector at an angle of 45°.
(a) In what direction does the pulse travel after reflection at both surfaces?
(b) What happens if the pulse is incident at some other angle?■

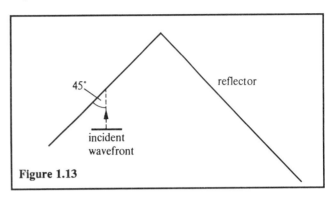

Figure 1.13

Q 1.23 Self-assessment question

(a) Figure 1.14 shows two sets of ripples which had a common point source. State the direction of travel of each wave pulse, and explain how this pattern has been formed.
(b) Give reasons why the plane wave shows a stronger contrast between dark and bright areas than the circular wave.
(c) Estimate the proportion of the total wave energy carried by the circular wave. ■

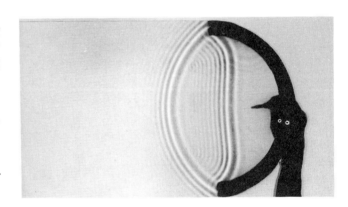

Figure 1.14

Refraction of waves

From qualitative observations in a ripple tank, the following points can be deduced.

1 Ripples travel more slowly in shallow water than in deep water.
2 The change in velocity produces a change in wavelength, but no change in frequency.
3 The change in velocity produces a change in the direction of the wavefront (except when the incident wavefront is parallel to the boundary). If the wave travels across a boundary into a medium in which the wave velocity is reduced, then the wavefronts become more nearly parallel to the boundary.

Q 1.24 Self-assessment question

A ripple tank is not levelled correctly and, when the water surface is disturbed at a point, a wavefront like that shown in figure 1.15 is produced. Describe how the tank is sloping and give reasons for your answer. ∎

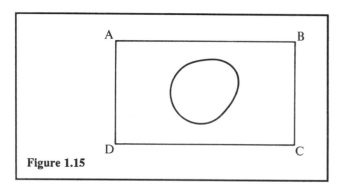

Figure 1.15

Q 1.25 Self-assessment question

Figure 1.16 shows a straight wavefront approaching a coastline. Assume that the sea has constant depth up to the line AB, but beyond AB the sea gets steadily shallower at a rate determined by the coastline shape.

(a) Sketch possible wavefronts as the waves travel to the beach.
(b) Draw in normals to these wavefronts to show the direction of energy flow, and explain why the sea is always calmer in a bay than on a headland. ∎

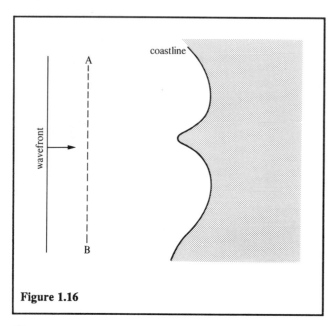

Figure 1.16

Q 1.26 Self-assessment question

Figures 1.17a and 1.17b show the refraction of ripples of different frequencies at the boundary of a shallow region. The angle of incidence is the same in each case, and so is the position of the black marker. Which frequency has been refracted most? ∎

The refraction of ripples of different frequency through different angles is an example of **dispersion**. This effect is produced when the speed of a wave in a medium depends on the wave frequency (and so also on its wavelength).

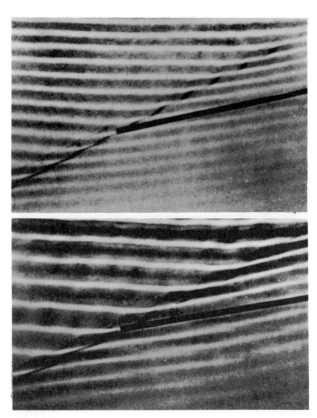

Figure 1.17

The medium is then described as a **dispersive medium**. A single complex shaped pulse in a rope may change its shape as it travels, because a rope is a dispersive medium. The complex pulse is made up of several sine wave pulses of different frequency, and these different frequencies travel at different speeds in the dispersive medium and cause the pulse shape to change. Fortunately, air is not a dispersive medium for sound waves, otherwise the shape of the sound wave would change as it travelled and sounds would 'sound' different at different distances from the source.

Interference

If circular ripples are generated by two dippers attached to the same vibrating bar, the superposed ripples form a steady pattern which we call an interference pattern. The vibrating dippers are described as **coherent** sources.

Sources are coherent if they have (a) the same frequency, and (b) a constant phase relationship (always in phase or always out of phase by the same amount). Also, if a pattern is to be observed, the two waves should have similar amplitudes. If the waves are transverse, the two coherent sources must produce displacements in the same plane (that is, the waves from each source must be polarised in the same plane or unpolarised).

Q 1.27 Development question*

Figure 1.18 shows circular waves radiating from two coherent sources vibrating in phase. The arcs show the positions of wavecrests at a particular instant.
(a) Where is the water level at each point marked with a dark circle at the instant recorded?
(b) Where will the water level be at each dark circle half a period later?

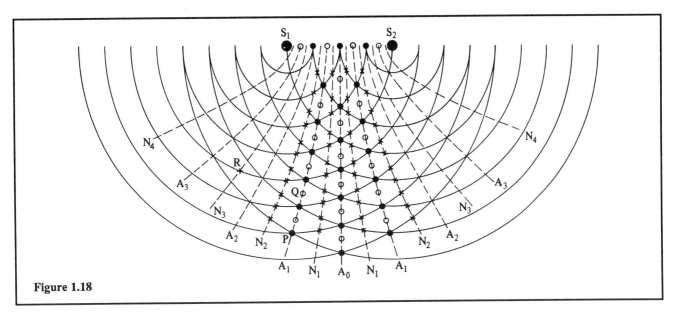

Figure 1.18

(c) What happens to the water level at each dark circle during one whole period? Does the water surface move in exactly the same way at each dark circle?

(d) Consider points marked with a blank circle, such as Q. How does the movement of the water surface at Q resemble that at points marked with dark circles, and how does it differ?

(e) What can you say about the amplitude of vibration at one point along a line, like A_1, of dark and blank circles? Are there any points on the surface which have a greater amplitude?

(f) A point in a wave where the vibration has maximum amplitude is called an antinode. A_0 and A_1 are **antinodal lines**. What is the path difference at point P from S_1 and S_2? Is the path difference the same for all other points along line A_1?

(g) Find the path difference for points along A_2 and A_3 and hence deduce a general expression for the path difference for any point on an antinodal line.

(h) Describe the state of the surface at points marked with a cross. Why can you describe the lines joining these points as nodal lines?

(i) Find the path difference at point R on line N_3 and hence deduce what the path differences must be along the nodal lines N_3 and N_4. ∎

Q 1.28 Self-assessment question

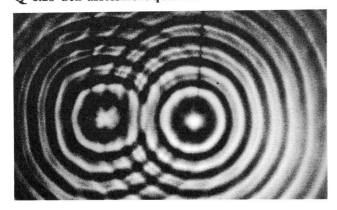

Figure 1.19a

Figure 1.19 shows interference patterns from two sources. The sources are the same distance apart in figures 1.19(a) and (b). The frequency is the same in figures 1.19(a) and (c).

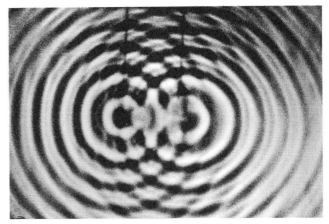

Figure 1.19b

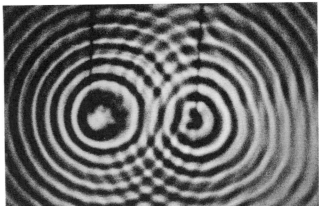

Figure 1.19c

Use the photographs to suggest how the separation x of adjacent nodal points, at a distance D from the source, depends on (i) the distance D, (ii) the source separation s, and (iii) the wavelength of the ripples λ. Hence, suggest a possible relationship between x and these quantities. ∎

Q 1.29 Self-assessment question

Two dippers placed 9 cm apart are vibrating in phase at a

frequency of 8 Hz. They produce ripples travelling at a speed of 24 cm s⁻¹. There are points along the line joining the dippers where the water is calm (nodes).

(a) How far from the mid-point of the line joining the sources is the nearest nodal point?
(b) How many nodes will there be along the line joining the sources?
(c) The dippers are now attached to separate vibrating bars so that they vibrate at the same frequency, 8 Hz, but are now out of phase by π rad (half a period). How does this affect the position and separation of the nodes?
(d) What will happen if the frequency of one dipper changes to 8.1 Hz? ■

Diffraction

Ripple tank experiments show that when a plane wave passes through an aperture the shape of the wavefront changes and the wave energy spreads round the corner of the obstacle. This effect is called **diffraction**, and it occurs whenever a wave passes an obstacle or passes through an aperture.

Q 1.30 Study question

(a) Describe how the shape of the diffracted wavefront and the distribution of the wave energy changes as the size of the aperture is steadily decreased. Are there any lines of calm water in the pattern?
(b) If waves of a range of frequencies pass through the same aperture, for which frequencies are the diffraction effects relatively more important?
(c) Sketch the diffracted wavefronts from an aperture whose width is one wavelength. ■

1.5 Wave speed

In this section we will study the factors which determine the speed of transverse waves in a string or wire. We begin by using another mechanical model of a wave, which enables us to study quantitatively the behaviour of a pulse, following up the work done in experiment WV 1.

E Experiment WV 3
Investigating pulse speed

In this experiment a wave pulse is sent through a line of trolleys joined together by springs. You will observe that the pulse speed depends upon the mass of the trolleys and the tension in the connecting springs.

In experiment WV3 you should have found that doubling the tension increases the pulse speed and that doubling the mass of each trolley reduces it. When the mass and the tension are both doubled, the wave speed is restored to its original value, since both quantities change the speed by the same factor.

Q 1.31 Self-assessment question

Explain why (i) increase in tension, and (ii) increase in mass have opposite effects on the wave speed. ■

We will now consider the mechanism by which a pulse travels along a string (or spring), and how one part of the string affects the next part. Figure 1.20a shows the positions of a wave pulse travelling along a string at two successive intervals of time. The solid line represents the position of the pulse at time t, and the broken line represents its position at time $(t + \Delta t)$. In the time interval Δt, point A on the string has moved to B and the leading edge of the pulse has moved along the string from A to A_1.

Q 1.32 Development question

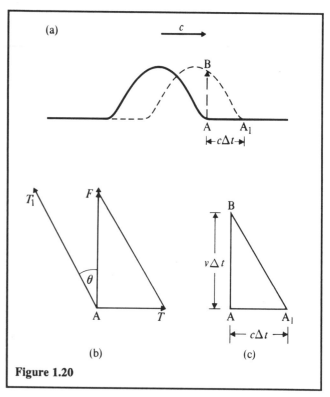

Figure 1.20

Figure 1.20b shows the forces acting on the leading edge A of the pulse. T_1 and T are the tensions on each side of A.
(a) Why is T_1 greater than T?
(b) Show that $T = T_1 \sin \theta$.
(c) Consider a small part of the string, of mass per unit length μ, which includes the leading edge A. A is accelerated from rest by the resultant force F and its average velocity during the time Δt is v, in the direction AB.
Show that the resultant force F is given by

$$F = T_1 \cos \theta = \frac{T}{\tan \theta}$$

(d) The leading edge A moves to A_1 in time Δt, as shown in figure 1.20c. Show that the mass of string that moves in the direction AB in time Δt is $\mu c \, \Delta t$, where c is the speed of the pulse along the string.
(e) Write down an expression for the rate of change of momentum of the string, $\Delta p/\Delta t$, and hence show from Newton's second law that $F = \mu c v$.
(f) With reference to figure 1.20c, show that

$$\tan \theta = \frac{c}{v}$$

(g) By rearranging the terms in the expressions derived in parts (c), (e) and (f), show that the speed of a transverse wave along a string is given by

$$c = \sqrt{\frac{T}{\mu}}$$

where T is the tension in the undisplaced part of the string.■

Notes. 1 You will not be expected to recall this proof in an examination.
2 The argument also applies to a periodic wave, which is just a series of pulses following one another at regular intervals.
3 This relationship can be verified experimentally using the trolley and spring model, but f must be the mass per unit length of the *system* (not the mass per unit length of the *springs*).

Q 1.33 Self-assessment question

(a) Use the method of dimensional analysis to verify the relationship between c, T and μ .(*Hint.* Assume that the relationship can be written in the form $c = k T^x \mu^y$, where x and y are numbers and k is a dimensionless constant.)
(b) A whip tapers towards the end. What happens to the speed of a pulse as it passes down the whip from the handle? Explain. ■

Q 1.34 Self-assessment question

(a) A string of length 20 m has a mass of 100 g, and is under a tension of 10 N. What will be the speed of a pulse along it? How long will it take the pulse to travel the length of the string?
(b) Transverse waves travel at a speed of 40 m s⁻¹ along a steel wire which is under a tension of 13.5 N. If the density of steel is 7.8 x 10³ kg m⁻³, what is the cross-sectional area of the wire? ■

Longitudinal waves

The second part of experiment WV 3 models the behaviour of longitudinal wave. A theoretical treatment of the factors determining the speed of such a wave is beyond the scope of this unit.

The equation giving the speed is of the same form as that for a transverse wave:

$$\text{wave speed} = \sqrt{\frac{\text{elastic property}}{\text{inertial property}}}$$

For a solid, the elastic property of the Young modulus E, and the inertial property is the density ρ giving the equation:

$$c = \sqrt{\frac{E}{\rho}}$$

For sound waves in a gas, the elastic property is the pressure P of the gas and the inertial property its density ρ. It can be shown that the speed of sound waves in a gas is given by

$$c = \sqrt{\frac{\gamma p}{\rho}}$$

where γ is the ratio of the principal specific or molar heat capacities of a gas (see the unit *Thermal properties*).

C Comprehension WV 1
The Big Wave

This is an account of the behaviour of the extraordinarily destructive phenomena called tsunamis and of the attempts made to predict their occurrence.

EXPERIMENT WV 1

Observing wave pulses

Apparatus

○ stopwatch or stopclock
○ metre rule
○ long spring
○ slinky spring

Figure 1.21

Figure 1.22

Longitudinal wave pulses

1 Place the slinky spring on a smooth surface. Pull one end of the spring sharply and keep pulling, moving the end at a steady speed. Watch the region of stretched spring spread along the slinky. The coil at the end of the slinky will not be acted on by the pulling force until the wave pulse reaches it. The speed of the moving parts of the spring is not the same as the speed of the wave pulse. What can you say in comparing these speeds?

2 Fix the slinky at one end and extend it along the smooth surface. By momentarily reducing the extension send a compression pulse down the slinky (figure 1.21). Observe and describe the motion of one coil of the slinky as a compression wave pulse passes down the slinky. Why is this kind of wave pulse called longitudinal?

Transverse wave pulses

1 Lay the long spring on a long table (or the corridor floor). Stretch the spring by fastening one end of an anchored string or by getting a partner to hold it.

2 Give the end a sideways flick to produce a single transverse pulse, as shown in figure 1.22 (the pulse is called *transverse* because parts of the spring move *across* the direction in which the pulse travels). Try producing pulses of different shape and amplitude.

3 Make observations which will enable you to answer the following questions.

(a) What happens to the size and shape of the pulse as it moves down the spring? Why?
(b) What decides the shape of a pulse?
(c) Does the pulse travel with a steady speed?
(d) Can one pulse catch up with another?
(e) What happens to the speed of a pulse if the tension in the spring is increased?
(f) What happens to a pulse when it is reflected from a fixed end?
(g) How does one particular coil move as the pulse passes down the spring? Illustrate your answer by sketching one particular pulse shape you have observed, and a graph showing how the position of a particular coil changes with time as this pulse passes.

4 Observe and describe what happens when two pulses of different shapes are sent along the spring in opposite directions at the same time.

5 Produce a continuous wave by oscillating the spring from side to side at a regular frequency. What happens to the wavelength (distance between adjacent wave crests) as the frequency changes?

6 Vary the frequency of a continuous wave until the waves sent out and reflected back combine to form a wave pattern which does not travel along the spring (this is called a standing wave).

continued

EXPERIMENT WV 1

Waves at a boundary

1 Fasten one end of the spring to a taut thread about 3 m long, and observe the reflection of a transverse pulse at this end. How does this compare with reflection at a fixed end?

2 Attach a small mass (e.g. about 100 g of lead) to one of the coils of the slinky or the long spring. This produces a 'discontinuity' in the wave medium (one heavy coil in the midst of many lighter ones). How is the wave energy reflected and transmitted at the discontinuity?

3 Join together the slinky and the long spring, and fix the long spring at its other end. Stretch the free end of the slinky and send a transverse wave pulse down it. Observe and describe what happens after the pulse reaches the boundary.

4 Keeping the springs joined, fix the end of the slinky and send a wave pulse down the long spring towards the slinky. Describe what happens after the pulse reaches the boundary.

Waves in a ripple tank

Apparatus

○ ripple tank kit, including motor,
  vibrator bar, dippers, reflectors,
  barriers and small perspex sheet
○ ripple tank illuminant
○ white paper screen

○ hand stroboscope
○ cell holder and U2 cells
○ rheostat, 0-15 Ω
○ leads

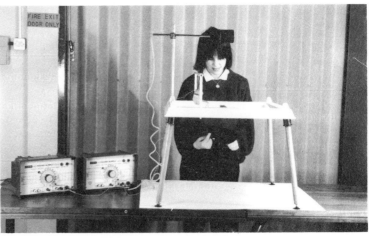

Figure 1.23

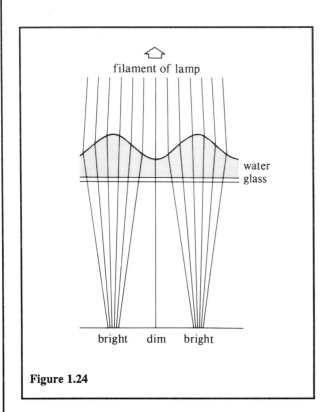

Figure 1.24

1 In this experiment you can use your observation of ripples as a model for waves in general. Try throughout to relate your observations to what you already know about the behaviour of sound and light.

2 Set up the ripple tank as in figure 1.23, with beaches or absorbers arranged to reduce wave reflection at the sides. Place a lamp about 50 cm above the tank and a white screen on the floor or bench below the tank. Pour in water to a depth of 5 mm. Level the tank. The two images of the lamp, due to reflection at the water surface and at the bottom of the tank, should coincide when the tank is level. Ripples in the tank act as lenses and produce bright and dark areas on the screen below the tank (figure 1.24). View the screen directly: do not look through the tank.

3 Observe wave pulses reflected from straight and curved reflectors. A circular wave pulse can be produced by touching the surface lightly or by dropping water from an eye dropper. A plane wave pulse is produced by placing a thick wooden rod in the tank and rolling it forward a little. Remove any bubbles clinging to reflectors in the tank. Record your observations using sketches, commenting on angles of incidence and reflection and the positions of images (sources of reflected waves).

continued

4 Observe the passage of a continuous wave from deep to shallow water. A continuous plane wave is produced by lowering the vibrator bar to touch the water surface. Place a glass or perspex sheet on steel washers in the tank and adjust the water level so that the perspex sheet is only just covered. Use a hand stroboscope to view the image of the ripples, adjusting the speed of rotation until the waves appear stationary.

5 The frequency of the wave remains constant, since the bar is vibrating at constant frequency. What effect has depth on the wavelength and wave velocity? Observe the refraction for different angles of incidence and different frequencies of the vibrator and note any significant observations.

6 Place two barriers parallel to the vibrator bar, in line with each other and with a gap of a few centimetres between them. Observe the passage of periodic plane waves through different sizes of aperture. Observe and record how the wave pattern beyond the aperture changes as the gap is narrowed. (The effect you are observing is called diffraction - the waves spread out beyond the aperture.)

7 Adjust the vibrator frequency and note the effect of changing the wavelength on the diffraction pattern. Which waves are diffracted most at a particular aperture, long or short? Is the diffraction effect determined by the actual size of the aperture, or by the size of the aperture relative to the wavelength of the waves? Test your answer by observation. Record any observed variation in the wave intensity (strength of the ripples) in different directions.

8 Fix two dippers to the vibrator bar, about 5 cm apart, and adjust the vibrator bar so that the dippers just dip into the water. Observe the pattern produced when two circular waves are superposed, from the two point sources vibrating in phase and with the same frequency.

Sketch the pattern of strong ripples and calm water, and observe the effect on this pattern of (i) changing the frequency of the dippers, (ii) changing the separation of the dippers.

9 Remove one of the dippers and set up a reflector so that it is 3 or 4 cm from the remaining dipper and at right angles to the vibrating bar. Explain how the pattern is produced, and say how the position of the reflector affects the pattern.

Investigating pulse speed

Apparatus

○ 12 dynamics trolleys (or 6 trolleys and 6 one kilogram masses)
○ 16 dowel rods
○ 20 springs (steel, expendable)
○ 20 springs, compression
○ G-clamp
○ stop watch

Figure 1.25

(a) Transverse pulse

1 Arrange the six dynamics trolleys as shown in figure 1.25, with the trolleys spaced out so that the springs are in tension.

2 Move the free-end trolley from side to side to send a transverse pulse down the line of trolleys. Time the interval between the start of the pulse and the return of the reflected pulse. Repeat four more times and record your results. Find the average time.

Note: Always move the trolley about the same point, i.e. keep the length of the trolley line constant so that the extension of each spring remains constant.

3 Investigate the effect of doubling the mass by attaching a second trolley to each trolley. (Use 1 kg masses if extra trolleys are not available.) Again, record the time for 5 pulses and find the average.

4 Remove the extra trolleys (or 1 kg masses) and attach a second pair of springs between each trolley as shown in figure 1.26. Repeat steps 2 and 3.

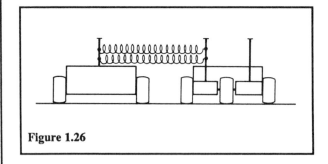

Figure 1.26

5 Calculate the pulse speed for each case.

6 What happens to the pulse speed when the tension is doubled?
What happens to the pulse speed when the mass of each trolley is doubled ?

What can you say about the pulse speed when the mass and tension are both doubled at the same time?

7 Why is this a reasonable model for the propagation of a transverse wave in a string? What do the springs and trolleys represent?

(b) Longitudinal pulse (optional)

1 Arrange the six trolleys as shown in figure 1.27. Each trolley is linked to the next one by means of a compression spring.

2 Send a compression pulse along the line of trolleys and calculate the speed of the pulse down the row of trolleys.

3 What happens to the speed of the pulse when the mass of each trolley is doubled?

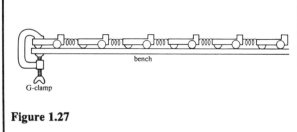

Figure 1.27

4 Why is this a reasonable model for the propagation of a longitudinal wave in air? What do the springs and trolleys represent?

Questions on objectives

Before you attempt these, check through the list of objectives for this topic and make sure that your notes on the topic have not left out anything important.

1 When a sinusoidal progressive mechanical wave of constant amplitude passes through a medium, which of the following statements are *true* and which are *false*?
(a) All particles vibrate with s.h.m. of the same frequency as the source.
(b) Particles vibrate with the same frequency but with different amplitudes.
(c) All particles have the same amplitude of vibration.
(d) Particles vibrate in phase with the source.
(e) Particles in the same wavelength have the same phase.
(f) The distance between adjacent particles in phase is constant.
(g) All particles within one wavelength have different phases.
(objectives 1 and 2)

2 Use the definitions of wavelength, frequency, and wave speed to obtain an equation relating these three quantities.

Sound can be recorded on tape which is magnetised as it passes a narrow gap between the poles of an electromagnet. The sound wave pattern is reproduced by the magnetising current in the coil. When the recorder is run with a tape speed of 17 cm s^{-1}, it is capable of recording and reproducing frequencies up to 10 kHz.
(a) What length of tape records one cycle of 10 kHz sound?
(b) Suggest a maximum size for the gap if the recorder is to reproduce 10 kHz sound accurately.
(c) What will the upper frequency limit be when the machine is run at 4.25 cm s^{-1}?
(objectives 2, 4)

3 Figure 1.28 shows six sketches of pulses in a heavy spring (left) joined to a lighter spring. Three of the sketches represent different instants in one event and the other three represent instants in a different event.
(a) Arrange the figures in two groups, in the correct sequences. Sketch the groups, indicating the direction of the wave pulse in each case.
(b) Explain how the sketches provide evidence that (i) wave energy is shared between transmitted and reflected pulses, (ii) the speed of the wave is greater in one spring than in the other, and (iii) the relative phase of reflection is determined by the direction of movement of the pulse when springs of different mass are joined.
(objective 5)

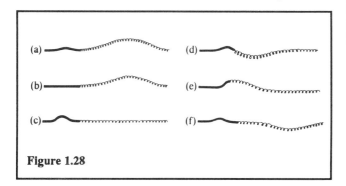

Figure 1.28

4 A circular wave pulse travels at a speed of 20 cm s^{-1} to a plane reflector placed 10 cm from the source.

Draw the wavefronts 0.7 s after the pulse left the source, indicating the scale of your diagram.
(objective 6)

5 Which of the following are altered when a travelling wave crosses a boundary between two media with different physical properties: velocity, frequency, wavelength, amplitude, phase?
(objectives 1, 7)

6 Earthquake waves are of two kinds, primary waves which are longitudinal and secondary waves which are transverse. Only one of these kinds of waves can travel through the earth's core. Suggest which one, and say what you can deduce about the earth's core.
(objective 3)

7 What is a dispersive medium?
(objective 7)

8 Figure 1.29 shows a graph of y against x for a travelling wave at a particular instant. Sketch the corresponding graph of y against t for point P, for one second after the instant shown
(objective 10)

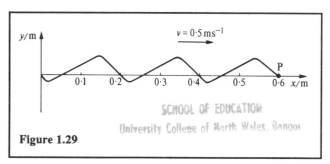

Figure 1.29

9 State the principle of superposition.

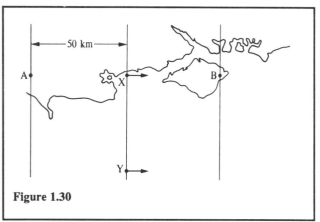

Figure 1.30

The map (figure 1.30) shows part of a coastline, with two land-based radio navigation stations A and B. Both stations transmit continuous sinusoidal radio waves with the same amplitude and same wavelength (200 m). A ship X, exactly midway between A and B, detects a signal whose amplitude is twice that of either station alone.
(a) What can be said about the signals from the two stations?
(b) The ship X travels to a new position by sailing 100 m in the direction shown by the arrow. What signal will it now detect? Explain this.
(c) A ship Y also starts at a position equidistant from A and

B and then travels in the direction shown by the arrow. Exactly the same changes to the signal received were observed as in the case of ship X in (b). Explain whether Y has sailed 100 m, more than 100 m, or less than 100 m.

(objectives 8 and 9)

Compare the time you took to complete this topic with the recommended time. Are you keeping up to schedule?
Do not forget to check your time after you have completed each topic.

TOPIC 2

Sound

Summary

This topic extends the use of the wave model, using a familiar wave type, sound. We shall describe and calculate how wave-energy may be bundled in time (beats) and in space (Doppler effect, standing waves). The idea of a bundle of energy is combined with the idea of a particle.

Dolphins are experts at using sonar echolocation. Find out how it works.

Objectives

When you have completed the work in this topic you should be able to:

1   Use the following scientific terms correctly: compression, rarefaction, beats, stationary (standing) wave, node, antinode, fundamental, harmonic, overtone, quality, resonance tube, end-correction.

2   Explain in terms of pressure variation and particle displacement, how a sound wave is propagated.

3   Draw and interpret diagrams which represent the variation of pressure and of particle displacement with time.

4   Describe and explain, with the aid of diagrams and appropriate experiments, the formation of stationary (standing) waves.

5   Recall and use the fact that the distance between consecutive nodes and consecutive antinodes is λ/2.

6   List the differences between progressive waves and stationary waves.

7   Describe and explain an experiment to determine the speed of sound in air.

8   Describe and explain the reflection, refraction and interference of sound waves.

9   Explain how beats are produced, and recall and use the equation for beat frequency.

10   Explain what is meant by the Doppler effect.

11   Derive and use expressions for the change in frequency of a wave motion when
(a) the source is moving relative to a fixed observer, and
(b) the observer is moving relative to a fixed source.

12   Outline a practical application of the Doppler effect.

13   Discuss the factors that affect the modes of vibration of vibrating strings, air columns and closed pipes.

14   Explain, with the aid of diagrams, the stationary wave patterns in closed and open tubes. Distinguish between displacement nodes, pressure nodes, displacement antinodes and pressure antinodes.

15   Perform and describe an experiment to determine the speed of sound in an air column (resonance tube method).

16   Use the equation $f = \dfrac{n}{2l} \sqrt{\dfrac{T}{\mu}}$

to solve problems on strings and wires.

Experiments

WV 4   Speed of sound in air   (0.75 hour)
WV 5   Interference of sound waves   (0.75 hour)

Experiments WV4 and WV5 can conveniently be carried out at the same time.

WV 6   Stationary waves on as string   (1 hour)
WV 7   Vibrations in an air column   (0.75 hour)

References

Akrill	Chapter 24
Bolton	Chapter 8
Duncan	Chapter 19
Muncaster	Chapters 30-35
Nelkon	Chapters 22 and 23
Whelan	Chapter 41

2.1 Nature of sound waves

Sounds originate from vibrating sources. Sound energy can be transmitted through gases, solids and liquids, but not through a vacuum. Sound is transmitted as a longitudinal progressive wave. As you observed, using a slinky in experiment WV 1, periodic longitudinal waves produce a series of compressions and rarefactions, travelling through the medium, which enable energy to be transmitted from source to receiver. Sound waves cause the ear-drum to vibrate and impulses are sent to the brain producing the sensation which we call 'sound'.

Sound waves are distinguished from other longitudinal waves by being *audible*. Sound waves are longitudinal progressive waves with frequencies between 20 Hz and 20 kHz. Audible frequency limits vary for different people, and the upper frequency limit decreases with age. You can find your own audible frequency range by connecting a loudspeaker to a signal generator and varying the frequency from 15 Hz up to that at which you can no longer hear any sound.

Longitudinal progressive waves with frequencies above 20 kHz are called **ultrasonic** waves. Ultrasonic waves and sound waves travel at the same speed. In air this speed is about 330 m s^{-1}. (The prefix *ultra* indicates 'higher than audible frequency', and must not be confused with the prefix *super* which is used in supersonic to indicate 'speeds greater than the speed of sound'.)

Ultrasonic waves with frequencies as high as 6×10^8 Hz (600 MHz) can be produced in a quartz crystal, using the piezo-electric effect (this effect causes a crystal to alternately shrink or expand when an alternating electric field is applied to it). A further study of the use of ultrasound is included in the topic Medical Physics, which appears in the *Student's resource book*.

Q 2.1 Self-assessment question

(a) What are the approximate wavelengths of the highest and lowest frequency sound waves?
(b) What is the wavelength of waves produced by an ultrasonic vibrator of frequency 10^8 Hz? ■

Representing sound waves

Figure 2.1a shows layers of particles in a medium in their undisturbed positions, and when displaced to new positions by the passage of a compression wave through the medium. Figure 2.1b shows the variation in particle displacement at different points in the medium. Particle displacement to the right is shown as positive displacement (upwards, on the graph).

We can observe particle displacement when a transverse wave travels along a spring; observing particle displacement when a longitudinal wave passes through air is much more difficult. The following exercise will help you to visualise the displacements which occur.

1 Cut a slit 2 mm wide and 90 mm long in a 100 mm x 150 mm card (or fasten two cards edge-to-edge with a 2 mm gap).

2 Place the card over figure 2.2 with the slit at the top of the diagram.

3 Move the card downward with a constant velocity. The parts of the sine curves that you see through the slit correspond to a row of particles along which a longitudinal wave is travelling. You should notice that each particle oscillates about its equilibrium position (it executes simple harmonic motion). All the particles have a similar motion, but within a wavelength each has a different phase, and regions of compression (higher pressure than ambient or normal) and rarefaction (pressure below ambient) travel from left to right with constant velocity.

Figure 2.2

Detectors of sound, like microphones, respond to the pressure variations which occur in the medium. It is therefore important to represent sound waves in terms of these pressure variations.

Q 2.2 Development question*

Figure 2.3 shows a graph of particle displacement y against distance x at a particular instant of time.

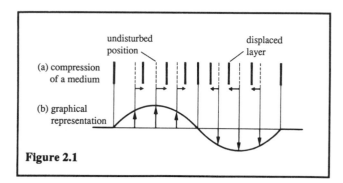

(a) compression of a medium — undisturbed position, displaced layer

(b) graphical representation

Figure 2.1

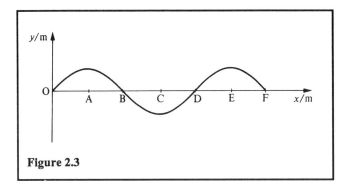

Figure 2.3

(a) In which regions have particles of the medium been displaced to the left, and in which to the right?
(b) At which points will the pressure be maximum (compression)?
(c) At which points will the pressure be minimum (rarefaction)?
(d) Where is the pressure normal?
(e) Sketch a graph of the pressure change Δp against distance x at the instant shown, marking in the points A-F. ■

The points of maximum pressure and maximum particle displacement do not coincide. The pressure is maximum or minimum where the displacement is zero. When the progressive wave is sinusoidal, the pressure curve has the same shape as the displacement curve, but is displaced by a quarter of a wavelength.

Atmospheric pressure is about 10^5 Pa and the wavelength of sound in air is about 1 m. For the loudest sound that we can tolerate, the pressure variation is approximately 30 Pa and the displacement of air molecules is about 10^{-5} m.

For the faintest sound that we can hear, the corresponding figures are 2×10^{-5} Pa and 10^{-11} m. The particle displacement for quiet sounds is, therefore, smaller than the wavelength of light (5×10^{-7} m), and for the very faintest of sounds it is even smaller than the diameter of an atom (10^{-10} m).

2.2 Properties of sound waves

Speed

The first attempts to measure the speed of sound in air directly were made in the sixteenth century. The basis of these methods was to measure the time interval which elapsed between seeing the flash of a distant gun and hearing the report.

Two contemporaries of Newton, the astronomers Flamsteed and Halley, measured the speed of sound between Greenwich Observatory and Shooters Hill, obtaining a value of 1142 feet per second (348 m s^{-1}).

Q 2.3 Self-assessment question

What were the main sources of error in this type of experiment? ■

Now, because refined and accurate methods of timing are available, you can measure the speed of sound directly by recording the transit time of sound waves over a very short distance of about 1 metre.

E Experiment WV 4
Speed of sound in air

This is a modern version of Flamsteed and Halley's experiment, using an oscilloscope to measure the speed of sound.

Reflection

When sound waves impinge on hard surfaces, most of the energy is reflected back, obeying the laws of reflection. At soft or porous surfaces, much of the wave energy is absorbed. If the reflecting surface is a long way from the observer, the reflected sound arrives some time after the waves travelling directly to the observer, and an echo is heard. The echo seems to be coming from another source: the virtual image formed by reflection. Echoes are useful for measuring sea depth (sonar depth finding), and the interior of the body can be investigated by obtaining echoes of ultrasonic waves.

In a large hall there are many reflecting surfaces close to an observer. The direct sound and the reflected sound cannot be distinguished, giving the impression that the original sound has been prolonged. It slowly fades away, as energy is absorbed in successive reflections. This effect is called **reverberation**, and the quality of the sound we hear is affected by these multiple reflections.

Q 2.4 Self-assessment question

How can you account for the fact that a 'rough' cliff face can produce a distinct sound image (an echo), whereas a highly polished surface is needed to produce a clear image when light is reflected? ■

Refraction

Sound waves can be refracted. Sound travels more rapidly in warm air than in cooler air. During the day the upper layers of the air are cooler than the layers nearer the earth whilst, at night, the opposite is true.

The speed of sound waves is increased, relative to a stationary observer, if the whole mass of air carrying the compressions is being blown towards her. We are all familiar with the difficulty of getting our voices to carry when we shout into the wind. The wind is producing refraction. This is because the wind speed is always low near the ground and increases with height.

Q 2.5 Discussion question

(a) Explain why sounds carry over long distances on a still, frosty night.
(b) Why does a hot still day seem quiet? ■

Interference

Sound waves can exhibit the phenomenon of interference. This can be observed by connecting two loudspeakers in parallel to a signal generator so that they oscillate in phase. The result of the superposition of the waves can be detected with a microphone and c.r.o., or by listening.

E Experiment WV 5
Interference of sound waves

In this experiment you will investigate a sound interference pattern and obtain data from which you can estimate the wavelength of sound waves and calculate the speed of sound in air.

Q 2.6 Self-assessment question

What will be the effect on a sound wave interference pattern if
(a) the pitch of both loudspeakers is lowered,
(b) the connections to one of the loudspeakers are reversed so that the two speakers oscillate out of phase? Give reasons for your answers. ∎

Beats

This effect is another example of superposition. It occurs when two waves of similar amplitudes but slightly different frequencies are superposed. The result is a periodic rise and fall in loudness.

Q 2.7 Study question

(a) Explain, with the help of a diagram, how beats are produced.
(b) What is meant by the term beat period?
(c) Derive an expression relating the beat frequency to the frequencies of the two superposed waves.
(d) How can beats be used to measure an unknown frequency? ∎

Q 2.8 Self-assessment question

A piano tuner sounds a calibrated tuning fork for middle C (256 Hz) at the same time as the middle C of the piano he is tuning. He hears beats of frequency 4 Hz.
(a) What are the possible frequencies of the piano string?
(b) What must he do to tune the string, and how will he know when it is in tune? ∎

2.3 The Doppler effect

The pitch of the note from a siren, of an ambulance or a fire engine, appears to change as it passes you. This apparent change in frequency is called the Doppler effect, and is due to the relative movement of source and observer. The effect is produced by a change in wavelength.

Moving source

Figure 2.4 represents wavecrests from a moving source. Successive positions of the source are represented by points S_1 to S_4. Wavefront 1 was emitted when the source was at S_1, wavefront 2 originated from point S_2, and so on.

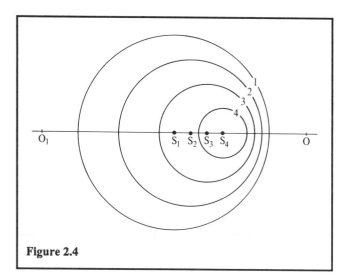

Figure 2.4

The wavefronts moving towards O are compressed, the wavefronts moving towards O_1 are spread out. However, the speed of the waves, c, is unchanged. It is not affected by the speed of the source since the wave speed is a property of the medium (and the waves 'forget about' the source as soon as they leave it).

Q 2.9 Development question

Source S travels with speeds v_s towards O and produces sound waves of frequency f_s and wave speed c.
(a) How far does the source travel in one second?
(b) How many wavefronts are produced in one second?
(c) What is the distance into which this one-second wavetrain travelling to O is packed?
(d) Show that the decreased wavelength at O, λ_o, is given by

$$\lambda_0 = \frac{c - v_s}{f_s}$$

(e) The observed frequency, f_o, is the number of wavelengths travelling past the observer in one second. Express f_o in terms of c and λ_o.

(f) Show that

$$f_0 = \left(\frac{c}{c - v_s}\right)f_s$$

(g) Show that, for an observer at O_1, the observed frequency is

$$\left(\frac{c}{c + v_s}\right)f_s \qquad \blacksquare$$

Q 2.10 Self-assessment question

A source emitting a note of frequency 600 Hz approaches a stationary observer at a constant velocity of one-fifth of the speed of sound in air, and passes him. Calculate the observed change in frequency as the source passes the observer. ∎

Suppose the source is moving along XY (figure 2.5) with a velocity v_s while the observer is stationary at O. When the source is at P, it is moving towards O with a component velocity along PO of $v_s \cos \theta$. It is this component of the velocity which determines the frequency heard at O.

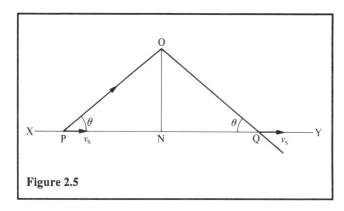

Figure 2.5

Q 2.11 Self-assessment question

Write down an expression for the apparent frequency f_o, in terms of the emitted frequency f_s, when the body is at
(a) point P,
(b) point N,
(c) point Q. ∎

Q 2.12 Self-assessment question

An observer's perpendicular distance from a point N on a railway track is 50 m. An express train moves along the track at a steady speed of 60 m s^{-1}, continuously sounding a whistle of frequency 500 Hz. The speed of sound in air is 340 m s^{-1}.
(a) What is the frequency heard by the observer when the distance x of the approaching train from the point N is
(i) 200 m, (ii) 100 m, (iii) 50 m, (iv) 20 m and (v) 0?
(b) Draw a graph to show how the frequency heard by the observer varies with the distance of the train from the point N, for both positive (train approaching) and negative (train receding) values of x.
(c) Sketch, using the same axes, the curve that would be obtained if the observer was closer to the track. ∎

Moving observer

In this case the wavelength λ is unchanged, but the movement of the observer affects the number of wavecrests received per second by the observer.

Q 2.13 Development question

If the source has an emitted frequency of f_s, a stationary observer receives f_s wavecrests per second.
(a) Express f_s in terms of λ and c.
(b) If the observer moves towards the source with speed v_o, how many extra wavecrests are received per second?
(c) The apparent frequency f_o is the total number of wavecrests received per second by the moving observer. Write down an expression for f_o.

(d) Hence show that $\quad f_0 = \left(\dfrac{c + v_0}{c}\right)f_s$

(e) If the observer moves away from the source, show that

$$f_0 = \left(\dfrac{c - v_0}{c}\right)f_s \qquad ∎$$

The relationships between the observed, or apparent, frequency f_o and the emitted frequency f_s can be summarised as follows.

For a moving source:

$$\frac{f_o}{f_s} = \frac{\text{velocity of waves relative to the medium}}{\text{velocity of waves relative to the source}}$$

For a moving observer:

$$\frac{f_o}{f_s} = \frac{\text{velocity of waves relative to the observer}}{\text{velocity of waves relative to the medium}}$$

The equations can be combined if both source and observer are moving relative to the medium.

Notes

1 In deriving the preceding equations, the velocities v_s, v_o and c were all assumed to be measured relative to the air or, more generally, to the medium in which the wave travels.
2 The Doppler effect occurs with electromagnetic waves. In this case there is no medium relative to which a velocity can be defined, and we can speak only of the relative velocity of the source and receiver.
3 The equations derived for sound waves can be used for electromagnetic waves if v_s and/or v_o is much less than c (3 x 10^8 m s^{-1} for e.m. waves). If v_o or v_s become comparable to c, different equations are needed.

Applications of the Doppler effect

Q 2.14 Self-assessment question

(a) A source of sound emits a note of frequency 1000 Hz (1 kHz). Suppose that the source moves at the speed of sound, c directly towards a stationary observer. Calculate the frequency of the note heard by the observer (i) as the source approaches, (ii) as the source recedes.
(b) If the source is stationary, and the observer moves directly towards the source with velocity c, calculate the frequency of the note heard by the observer (i) as he approaches the source, (ii) as he recedes from the source.
(c) Comment on your results. ∎

Q 2.15 Self-assessment question

Sounding its horn, a car moves away from a stationary observer at a steady speed of 5 m s^{-1} towards a plane reflecting wall.
The frequency of the note emitted by the horn is 400 Hz, and the speed of sound in air is 340 m s^{-1}. What is the frequency of the beats heard by the observer? ∎

The Doppler effect for electromagnetic waves can be used in tracking an artificial satellite (figure 2.6). The satellite emits a radio signal of constant frequency f_s.

The signal received on the ground from the satellite is combined with a constant signal, also of frequency f_s, generated in the receiver. This gives rise to beats.

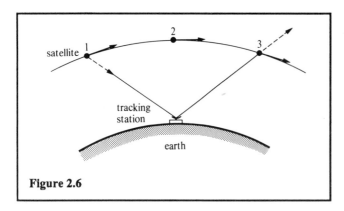

Figure 2.6

Q 2.16 Self-assessment question

(a) What happens to the beat frequency Δf as the satellite moves from position 1 to position 3?

(b) If v_s is the component of the satellite's velocity towards the receiving station, show that

$$\frac{\Delta f}{f_s} \approx \frac{v_s}{c}$$

(Assume that Δf is small, and f_o is, therefore, approximately equal to f_s.) ■

A similar technique, using the Doppler effect and beats, is employed to detect the movement or measure the speed of a reflecting surface. Emitter and receiver are placed together near the moving surface. Waves reflected back to the source from an approaching target surface will have an increased frequency. This changed frequency is mixed with the original emitted frequency to obtain the beat frequency, which depends on the speed of the reflecting surface.

Q 2.17 Study question

If a reflecting surface travels towards a stationary emitter/receiver with speed v, show that the detected change in frequency, Δf, is given by

$$\Delta f \approx \frac{2v}{c} f_s$$

where f_s is the emitted frequency. (Hint: consider the moving reflector as a moving 'observer' receiving waves from a stationary source, and then as a moving 'source' emitting to a stationary receiver.) ■

The Doppler-shift frequency Δf can be used to detect a foetal heart beat, if ultrasonic waves are reflected from the moving surface of the heart. The ultrasonic frequency can be adjusted to produce a value of Δf which is in the audible range, producing sound in the detector earphones. Waves reflected from stationary structures in the body will undergo no Doppler shift and the observer will hear nothing. Reflections from a beating heart will produce a varying tone in the earphones.

Speed detectors used by police measure car speeds using the Doppler-shift frequency with electromagnetic waves (radar).

Q 2.18 Self-assessment question

Microwaves of wavelength 100 mm are transmitted from a source so as to strike a car which is approaching the source. The reflected wave is found to give a beat frequency of 200 Hz when superposed on the transmitted wave. The speed of electromagnetic waves is 3×10^8 m s^{-1}. Calculate the speed of the approaching car. ■

The Doppler effect for light waves is important in astronomy. Analysis of the spectra of light from distant stars shows shifts in the frequency of spectral lines compared to spectra from the same elements on earth. These can be interpreted as Doppler shifts due to the motion of the stars. For a star travelling away from the observer with speed v, $\Delta f/f = v/c$.

2.4 Stationary waves

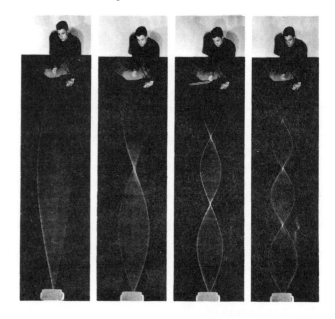

Figure 2.7

We have seen that when waves are sent down a rope, which is fixed at one end, the waves will be reflected. For certain frequencies the incident and reflected waves produce patterns, such as those illustrated in figure 2.7. In this section we will consider how this type of wave, called a **stationary** (or standing) wave, is produced.

Transverse stationary waves are produced in the strings, and longitudinal stationary waves in the air columns, of musical instruments. Stationary waves, due to oscillating electrons, occur in radio and television aerial systems tuned to incoming radio waves. Electrons have wave properties. The fact that an atom has definite energy levels can be accounted for by assuming that the electron in the atom behaves like a stationary wave (see the Unit *Electrons and the nucleus*).

E Experiment WV 6
Stationary waves on a string

The aim of this experiment is to produce a stationary wave pattern on a string and investigate the effect of changing the driving frequency and tension in the string.

Formation of a stationary wave

The stationary wave pattern set up in experiment WV 6 was the result of the **superposition** of a wave travelling out from the vibrator and a wave reflected back, at a rigid boundary, along the string in the opposite direction. The pattern is the result of the superposition of two waves of *equal frequency* and *amplitude* travelling along the *same line* with the *same speed* but in *opposite directions*.

Q 2.19 Development question*

Figure 2.8 shows the displacement-distance graphs of two sinusoidal waves, R and L, of the same amplitude and frequency. R (shown by the thin line) is travelling to the right at 0.5 m s⁻¹ and L (shown by the broken line) is travelling to the left at the same speed. The thick line shows the resultant wave shape, at the instant shown ($t = 0$), formed by superposition. The amplitude of each wave is 0.5 m and the wavelength 2.0 m.
(a) Copy these graphs on a sheet of graph paper.

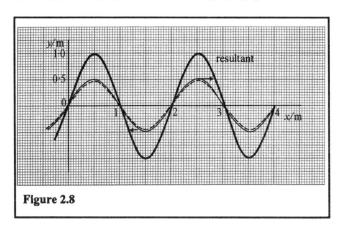

Figure 2.8

(b) Underneath your diagram draw graphs to show the positions of R and L after a time interval of 1.0 s and their resultant at this instant.
(c) Repeat (b) to show the situations when $t = 2.0$ s and when $t = 3.0$ s.
(d) Now draw the situations at $t = 0.5$ s and $t = 2.5$ s.
(e) On a single diagram, show the resultant wave shapes that you obtained in (b), (c) and (d). Your diagram will show some of the shapes taken by the resultant wave in this time interval.
(f) Which points in the medium appear to have (i) zero displacement and (ii) maximum displacement during this interval of time?
(g) What is the distance between these positions?
(h) How does this distance compare with the wavelength of the progressive wave? ■

Nodes and antinodes

The important result of this type of superposition is that the waves produced do not move through the medium (e.g. string), as shown in figure 2.9. There are points on the string which have zero displacement. Such points are called **nodes**, N, and are separated by a distance of λ/2, where λ is the common wavelength of the waves. Also, there are points which have maximum displacement, called **antinodes**, A. These are also separated by a distance λ/2.

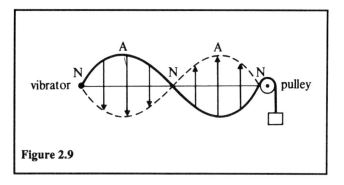

Figure 2.9

Q 2.20 Self-assessment question

(a) Draw graphs to show how the displacement of a particle at (i) a nodal point and (ii) an antinodal point varies with time.
(b) How do the particles in the medium between adjacent nodes move? Comment on their phase relationships and amplitudes.
(c) How does the movement of a particle on one side of a node differ from that of a particle on the other side? ■

Q 2.21 Study question

(a) Make a summary of the differences between progressive waves and stationary waves. You should comment on the following features: (i) amplitude, (ii) frequency, (iii) wavelength, (iv) phase, (v) waveform, (vi) energy.
(b) Make brief notes on experiments to illustrate the differences between (i) transverse waves and longitudinal waves, and (ii) progressive waves and stationary waves. ■

Stationary waves on a string

We will now consider why a stationary wave pattern in a string of fixed length only occurs at certain frequencies. When a single pulse is reflected at a rigid boundary, it is reflected upside down - a pulse in the form of a crest is reflected as a trough and *vice versa*. We say there is a phase change of π rad or half a cycle. When a progressive or travelling wave runs along the string, the wave is reflected at the rigid boundary and the two sets of waves combine to form a stationary wave in the string. Figure 2.10 illustates what happens at the rigid boundary. At time $t = 0$ the wave is just arriving at the boundary.

Now let us consider what happens when the reflected wave gets back to the other end of the string. In this case we are considering it as fixed (e.g. rope held by hand or string passing over pulley). This constitutes a boundary: reflection will take place and the wave will travel back down the string. The reflected wave will combine with new waves being fed in from the source. If it is in step with these waves, they will reinforce each other and build up a wave of larger amplitude. If it is not in step, they will partially or completely cancel each other out, depending on the phase relation between the two sets of waves.

The frequency of the source can be changed (as in experiment WV6) until a stationary wave pattern is formed at a particular frequency f. The time taken for the wave to travel along the string depends upon the wave speed c (which is determined by the tension and the mass per unit length) and the distance l between the two fixed ends. Because there are two phase changes, the reflected wave will be in phase with the new waves if the time taken to travel twice the length of the string is nT, where T is the periodic time. Therefore

$$l = \frac{cnT}{2} = \frac{n\lambda}{2}$$

as there must be an integral number of nodes, spacing $\lambda/2$ on the string.

As the frequency of the source approaches the natural frequency of the string, stationary waves are formed. When the frequencies exactly coincide, the amplitude of the stationary waves will be maximum - this is called **resonance**.

Alternatively, if the source frequency cannot be adjusted, stationary wave patterns can be produced by changing the natural frequency of the string (for example, by changing l or T).

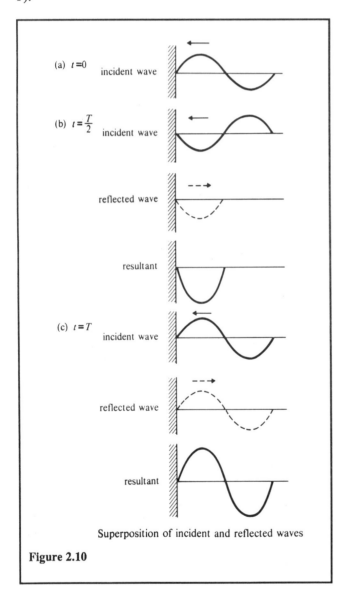

Superposition of incident and reflected waves

Figure 2.10

Q 2.22 Self-assessment question

A string is fixed at both ends. Trace the passage of a progressive wave, starting at one end, along the cord and explain how a stationary wave pattern of large amplitude, as in figure 2.11, is produced. ■

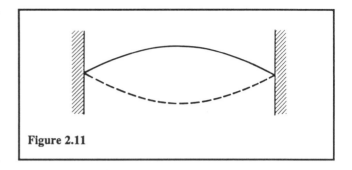

Figure 2.11

Q 2.23 Self-assessment question

(a) Show that for a string of length l, which is fixed at both ends,

$$f = n\,\frac{c}{2l}$$

where f is the natural frequency of the string and n is a whole number.
(b) Explain what happens for values of $f = n(c/2l)$. To what type of vibration is the string being subjected.
(c) Explain why, in practice, (i) there is not zero displacement at the nodes and (ii) it is possible to obtain a stationary wave pattern even if f is not an integral multiple of $c/2l$. ■

Q 2.24 Self-assessment question

A vibrator is driven from the a.c. mains at a frequency of 50 Hz and has a string under a tension of 4.9 N attached to it. The other end of the string is fixed (but adjustable). The mass per unit length of the string is 1.0×10^{-3} kg m^{-1}.
(a) What is the speed of a transverse wave along the string?
(b) Calculate the length of string which will show a stationary wave pattern with three antinodes. ■

Stationary waves in air

Stationary waves can be obtained in air by using a tube which is either closed or open at one end. The air at the other end is vibrated by means of a loudspeaker which is electrically driven by a signal generator. Progressive longitudinal waves travel down the tube, are reflected, and superimpose with the incident wave to give rise to a longitudinal stationary wave. The apparatus is sometimes referred to as Kundt's tube (although he did not use a signal generator - his source of longitudinal waves was a vibrating rod).

Background reading

You can use one of your textbook references to read of Kundt's investigation of the vibration of a column of air in a tube, how the measurement of wavelength is made and how this can be used to calculate the speed of sound in air.

In the investigation 'dust' or pollen is used to find the nodes, where there is no vibration. Between the nodes, the amplitude of the vibration varies with location. The following exercise will help you to visualise a longitudinal stationary wave.

Q 2.25 Study question

1 Cut a slit 2 mm wide and 90 mm long in a 100 mm x 150 mm card (or fasten two cards edge-to-edge with a 2 mm gap).

2 Place the card over figure 2.12 with the slit at the top of the diagram.

3 Move the card downward with a constant velocity. The parts of the curves which appear in the slit correspond to the vibrations of the particles in a longitudinal stationary wave.■

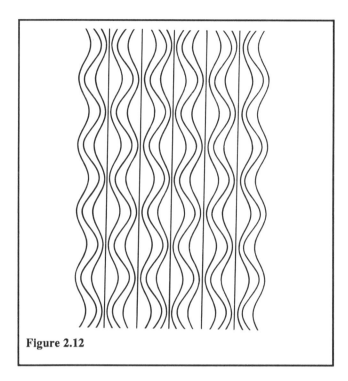

Figure 2.12

A stationary wave set up in an air column exists as both a stationary wave of particle displacement and as a stationary wave of pressure variation. When a stationary sound wave is illustrated, it is important to distinguish between these two sets of waves.

C Computer program
Stationary waves

If your school has appropriate software, this can show effectively how a stationary wave is built up.

Q 2.26 Self-assessment question

What can you say about the pressure at (i) a point where the particles are crowded together, and (ii) a point where the particles are removed in both directions? ■

Figure 2.13 illustrates the variation of longitudinal particle displacement with location at two instants of time, t and $(t + T/2)$. The length of arrow indicates the amplitude of the particle displacement and the direction shown is for time t.

Q 2.27 Self-assessment question

Copy figure 2.13. Using the same scale for the x-axis, draw graphs to illustrate the pressure variation at these two instants of time. ■

The pressure variation is always a maximum at a displace-

ment node and is always zero at a displacement antinode. In the next experiment, a microphone is used to locate the positions of maximum and zero pressure variation in a stationary wave in free air.

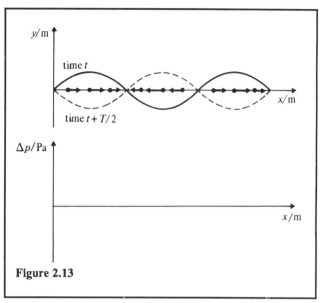

Figure 2.13

2.5 Vibrations in strings

The vibrating string (struck, plucked or bowed) forms the basis of probably the most important class of musical instruments. In this section we will be concerned with the factors that determine the frequency and quality of the note produced by a vibrating string.

When a string vibrates, progressive transverse waves travel along the string to both ends, which are fixed. Here they are reflected and combine with the incident waves. A stationary wave pattern is formed for waves whose wavelengths are correctly matched to the length of the string and the sound produced is transmitted to the surrounding air.

Q 2.28 Self-assessment question

How is the intensity of a note produced by a string in a musical instrument increased (without the aid of electrical amplifiers)? ■

Modes of vibration

The simplest mode of vibration of a string occurs when it is plucked at the centre and there is an antinode between the fixed ends (nodes) of the string, as shown in figure 2.14(a).

Q 2.29 Development question

(a) The length of the string is l, the tension in the string is T and its mass per unit length is μ. Show that the frequency of the fundamental note is given by

$$f_1 = \frac{1}{2l} \sqrt{\frac{T}{\mu}}$$

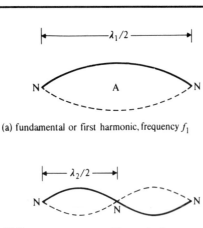

(a) fundamental or first harmonic, frequency f_1

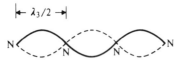

(b) first overtone or second harmonic, frequency f_2

(c) second overtone or third harmonic, frequency f_3

(d) third overtone or fourth harmonic, frequency f_4

Modes of vibration of a string

Figure 2.14

These three statements are known as the laws of vibration of stretched strings or Mersenne's laws (published by him in 1636). They can be verified experimentally using a sonometer, or by the arrangement used in experiment WV 6 (Melde's experiment).

Q 2.31 Study question

Make brief notes on how you would verify experimentally the relationship between the frequency of the fundamental note emitted by a stretched wire and (i) its tension, (ii) its length, (iii) its mass per unit length. You should include details of the experimental procedure, the results you would record and the graphs that you would plot. ■

Q 2.32 Self-assessment question

(a) How does the frequency of a wire of given material and given length under a fixed tension depend upon its diameter?
(b) A stretched steel wire of diameter 5.0×10^{-4} m is supported at two points 0.30 m apart. Calculate the tension that must be applied to make its fundamental frequency 500 Hz. (Density of steel $= 7.8 \times 10^3$ kg m^{-3}.) ■

Q 2.33 Self-assessment question

A copper wire is stretched horizontally so that its centre is between the poles of two strong magnets. The distance between the supports is 0.75 m and the mass per unit length of the wire is 1.8×10^{-3} kg m^{-1}. The wire carries an alternating current of frequency 50 Hz.
(a) The current is switched on and the tension in the wire is adjusted until a position is reached when the wire is seen to be vibrating in one loop with large amplitude. Explain why this happens.
(b) Calculate the tension in the wire. ■

(b) When the string is plucked at a point which is a quarter of the string's length from one end, it vibrates as shown in figure 2.14(b). Show that the frequency f_2 of the note is given by $f_2 = 2f_1$.
(c) Figures 2.14(c) and 2.14(d) show other possible modes of vibration. Write down a general expression for the frequencies produced. ■

Q 2.30 Self-assessment question

A wire is tuned to vibrate at a frequency of 1 kHz. What will the fundamental frequency of vibration be if

(a) its tension is doubled (assume length and mass per unit length unchanged),
(b) its length is doubled (assume tension is still doubled and mass per unit length unchanged),
(c) its mass per unit length is doubled (assuming tension and length are still doubled)? ■

Laws of a vibrating string

From the above discussion, it follows that

$$f_1 \propto \frac{1}{2l}, \text{ if } T \text{ and } \mu \text{ are constant}$$

$$f_1 \propto \sqrt{T}, \text{ if } l \text{ and } \mu \text{ are constant}$$

$$f_1 \propto \sqrt{\mu}, \text{ if } T \text{ and } l \text{ are constant}$$

Pitch

A sound is said to have a pitch if it has associated with it a distinct recognisable musical note or tone. Pitch is the musical term describing what we hear, while frequency is a scientific term describing what we can measure. A certain pitch corresponds directly to a certain fundamental frequency. (On the other hand, a noise is a sound which has no identifiable pitch.)

The most important interval of pitch is an octave - the interval between two notes whose frequencies are in the ratio 1:2. The octave can be subdivided into a scale of notes. Different cultures and ages have evolved different scales - the one we are familiar with is the diatonic scale represented in table 2.1. This is a scale of notes which can begin on any frequency and proceed, by the intervals shown, to the octave above. In music, the term interval represents a frequency *ratio*.

Q 2.34 Self-assessment question

(a) Explain the term quality and state the physical properties of sound waves on which it depends.
(b) What is meant by the fundamental frequency? Distinguish between harmonics and overtones. ■

Table 2.1

	C	D	E	F	G	A	B	C
Note	doh	re	me	fah	soh	lah	te	doh
Frequency	256							
Frequency ratio of adjacent notes		$\frac{9}{8}$	$\frac{10}{9}$	$\frac{16}{15}$	$\frac{9}{8}$	$\frac{10}{9}$	$\frac{9}{8}$	$\frac{16}{15}$

Q 2.35 Self-assessment question

Complete the line in table 2.1 giving the frequencies. ∎

Q 2.36 Self-assessment question

How is it possible to play a scale on a guitar or violin using
(a) only one string,
(b) two or more strings? ∎

Quality of a musical note

It is not difficult to distinguish notes of the same pitch played on different instruments. Analysis of such notes shows that the quality of the sound heard depends on the shape of the waveform of the vibrations reaching the listener. Several factors affect this waveform.

When a guitar string is plucked, the stationary wave produced in the string does not have a simple sine wave shape. The waveform has a pointed shape at first and changes its shape as the vibrations die away. Any regularly repeated wave pattern, however complex, can be built up by adding together a series of sine waves with frequencies which are all multiples of a fundamental frequency. Figure 2.15 shows how a complex waveform is produced by adding together sine waves of frequencies f, $2f$ and $3f$.

The frequencies which are integral multiples of the fundamental are called **harmonics**. The particular shape of the wave depends on which harmonics are present and their relative intensities. The vibrating guitar string produces a complex vibration which includes the fundamental and a whole series of harmonics, and the particular waveform can be changed by plucking at a different place or in a different way. These many frequencies produced by the string act as forcing vibrations to produce resonant vibrations of the wood of the guitar body and the air inside it. All frequencies higher than the fundamental are called **overtones**. Some may definitely not be harmonics, like the high-pitched squeals produced by a badly played violin which are caused by inharmonic torsional oscillations of the string.

⊏ Computer program
Sine waves

Check if you have available a computer program to illustrate sine waves.

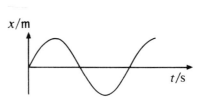

fundamental (frequency f, amplitude a)

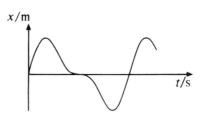

fundamental (frequency f, amplitude a)
+ second harmonic (frequency $2f$, amplitude $a/2$)

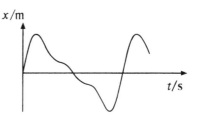

fundamental (frequency f, amplitude a)
+ second harmonic (frequency $2f$, amplitude $a/2$)
+ third harmonic (frequency $3f$, amplitude $a/4$)

Complex waveform as the sum of harmonic sine waves

Figure 2.15

2.6 Vibrations in air columns

The vibrating column of air in a tube or pipe is the basis of many forms of musical instrument. In this section we will study the formation of stationary waves in closed and open pipes and discuss the different modes of vibration.

The air can be set vibrating in many ways: for example, by blowing air over an edge or by means of a vibrating reed. Longitudinal progressive waves travel from the source of disturbance, are reflected back from the other end of the pipe and superimpose with incident waves to form a longitudinal stationary wave. Resonance will occur only for those wavelengths that fit the length of the pipe.

Q 2.37 Self-assessment question

(a) If you blow across the mouth of a milk bottle or boiling tube which is partially filled with water, a note is produced. Does the pitch of this note depend upon (i) how hard you blow, (ii) the depth of the water in the tube?
(b) What happens to the pitch of the note produced by blowing over the end of an open cardboard tube when you close the other end with your hand? ∎

(If you do not know the answers, try out the simple experiments described in the questions.)

We will now consider the factors that determine the lowest frequency (i.e. the fundamental mode of vibration) produced by a closed pipe (that is, one that is closed at one end) and an open pipe (that is, one that is open at both ends).

Q 2.38 Development question

Consider compression pulses travelling down a closed tube and an open tube.
(a) How will the pulse be reflected at (i) the closed end, (ii) the open end?
(b) When the pulses arrive back at the other end, how will they be reflected?
(c) For resonance to occur, what can you say about the phase relationship between the incident pulse from the source and the reflected pulse?
(d) What can you say about the displacement amplitude at (i) the closed end, (ii) the open end?
(e) What can you say about the excess pressure amplitude at (i) the closed end, (ii) the open end?
(f) Draw diagrams to illustrate the longitudinal stationary wave particle displacement for the first position of resonance in (i) the closed tube, (ii) the open tube.
(g) Derive expressions for the fundamental frequency of (i) the closed tube, (ii) the open tube, in terms of the length l of the tube and the speed of sound c. (Assume that the position of the displacement antinode coincides with the end of the tube.)
(h) Hence show that the fundamental frequency of the open pipe is twice that of a closed pipe of the same length. ■

Q 2.39 Study question

(a) Explain why the effective length of the vibrating air column exceeds the length of the pipe.
(b) What is meant by the end-correction? ■

E Experiment WV 7
Vibrations in an air column

In this practical work you will study the resonant vibrations of an air column and measure the speed of sound in air.

Q 2.40 Study question

(a) Draw diagrams to show the position of displacement nodes and displacement antinodes in two organ pipes of the same length, one with a closed end and the other with an open end, when they are sounding (i) the fundamental frequency, (ii) the first overtone, (iii) the second overtone.
(b) Show, neglecting end-corrections, that (i) for the closed pipe, the overtone frequency f_n is given by $f_n = (2n + 1)f_o$ where f_o is the fundamental frequency of the closed pipe and $n = 1, 2, 3, \ldots$, and (ii) for the open pipe, the overtone frequency f_n^1 is $f_n^1 = (n + 1)f_o^1$ where f_o^1 is the fundamental frequency of the open pipe.
(c) Account for the fact that the note from an open pipe gives a richer note than that from a closed pipe. ■

Q 2.41 Self-assessment question

(a) Two organ pipes with closed ends are sounded together, and eight beats per second are heard. If the shorter pipe is 0.50 m long, what is the length of the other pipe?
(b) A loudspeaker is connected to a signal generator and placed over the open end of a vertical tube 0.40 m long which is open at the other end. At what frequencies will resonance occur, as the frequency of the note emitted is increased from 400 Hz to 1800 Hz?

(You may ignore any end corrections. The speed of sound in air is 340 m s^{-1}.) ■

Q 2.42 Self-assessment question

The results shown in table 2.2 were obtained using a resonance tube closed at one end. The driving force was a loudspeaker which was connected to a signal generator. f is the frequency of the signal generator and l is the length of the air column at which the first position of resonance occurred for that frequency. The temperature of the air was 290 K.

Table 2.2

f/Hz	500	550	600	650	700
l/mm	155	138	130	112	103

(a) Plot these results so as to obtain a straight line graph.
(b) Explain why the graph does not pass through the origin and estimate the radius of the tube.
(c) Calculate the speed of sound in air at a temperature of 273 K. ■

Wind instruments

To produce sound from a wind instrument, a driving vibration sets up resonant vibrations in the air column. The complex sound produced contains a whole series of harmonics though, as we have discovered, only the odd harmonics can be present in the sound from a closed pipe.

The driving vibration in an oboe is provided by making a double reed vibrate, a trumpeter uses his lips to produce this driving vibration and in organ pipes a sharp edge or metal reeds are used. The quality of the sound produced will depend on:

1 the shape of the vibrating air column,

2 the material of the instrument and the thickness of the material,

3 the kind of driving vibration used,

4 the player, who controls the air pressure and the pressure on the vibrating reed.

How is the pitch varied?

A bugler can produce only a few notes from his simple instrument. By the way he blows (increasing his lip pressure)

he can make the air column produce not only the fundamental but higher and higher harmonics in the series f, $2f$, $3f$, etc., but he cannot produce a note of frequency $3f/2$.

The complete range of notes can only be produced by using a trumpet, in which the length of the pipe can be varied by opening one or more of the three valves on the instrument.

In other wind instruments the pitch of the fundamental frequency is controlled by opening and closing holes along the length of the air column though, even in this case, higher frequencies can be obtained by the way the player blows.

Speed of sound in air

Apparatus

○ cathode ray oscilloscope
○ metre rule
○ microphone
○ amplifier
○ loudspeaker
○ leads

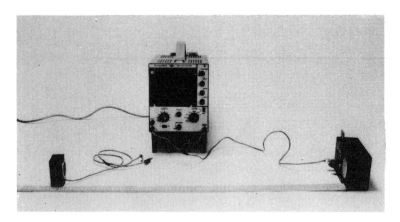

Figure 2.16

Note. If you have not used a cathode ray oscilloscope you should familiarise yourself with its controls before starting the experiment. (The controls of a typical c.r.o. are described in the unit *Electronic systems*. The manufacturer's handbook will give details for the particular oscilloscope you are using.)

Investigating the sweep output

1 In order to carry out this experiment the oscilloscope must have an output terminal (labelled 'sweep output' or 'probe test') from the calibrated time base. Check this is available on the c.r.o. you use.

2 Set up the apparatus as shown in figure 2.16. Connect the sweep output and the earth terminals of the c.r.o. to the input of the amplifier. Connect the output of the amplifier to the loudspeaker.

3 Set the time base at a slow setting (e.g. 100 ms cm⁻¹). What do you observe?

Measurement of speed

1 Connect the microphone to the input and earth terminals of the c.r.o.

2 Set the Y-gain control to its maximum setting (e.g. 0.1 V cm⁻¹) and the time base at a faster speed (e.g. 1 ms cm⁻¹).

3 When the microphone is placed closed to the loudspeaker a pattern should be obtained on the screen (figure 2.17). Move the microphone away from the loudspeaker. The position of the trace should change. Give a reason for this.

Note. You may have to adjust the gain control of the amplifier.

4 Move the microphone through a measured distance (e.g. one metre), record the length x on the c.r.o. and hence find the time taken for the sound waves to travel a distance of one metre.

5 Repeat the experiment several times and find an average value for the speed of sound in air.

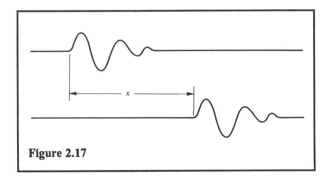

Figure 2.17

EXPERIMENT WV 5

Interference of sound waves

Apparatus

○ signal generator
○ 2 loudspeakers
○ microphone
○ cathode ray oscilloscope
○ leads
○ metre rule

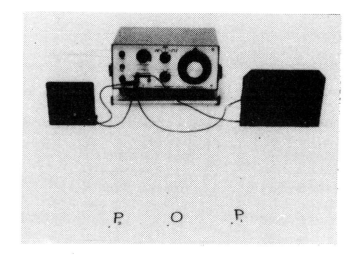

Figure 2.18

Note. If possible, carry out this experiment outside the laboratory. If you do carry it out indoors, keep the sound at a low volume.

1 Place the two loudspeakers about 2 m apart, as shown in figure 2.18. Connect them in parallel to the low impedance output of the signal generator. The output of the signal generator should be set at about 400 Hz.

2 Stand at the central position O in front of the loudspeakers, then walk back and forth along a line parallel to a line joining the two speakers, and listen for loud and quiet places. Why does this observation provide evidence for the wave nature of sound?

Note. If the central position O turns out to be a place of minimum intensity, reverse the connections to one of the loudspeakers. This will make it a place of maximum intensity.

3 Locate the first position, P_1, of maximum intensity on one side of O. What can you say about the waves which arrive at P_1 from the two loudspeakers S_1 and S_2? Measure the distances $P_1 S_1$ and $P_1 S_2$, and calculate the path difference $(P_1 S_1 - P_1 S_2)$. How is this distance related to the wavelength of the sound waves?

4 Using the relationship $c = f\lambda$, estimate a value for the speed of sound in air.

5 Repeat steps 3 and 4 for the first point of maximum intensity, P_2, on the other side of O.

6 Repeat the experiment, using a microphone connected to a c.r.o. to detect the variation in amplitude of the sound at different places about 1 m from the loudspeakers. Arrange the speakers about 0.5 m apart and use a frequency of 4 kHz.

Stationary waves on a string

Apparatus

○ signal generator
○ vibrator
○ pulley
○ string

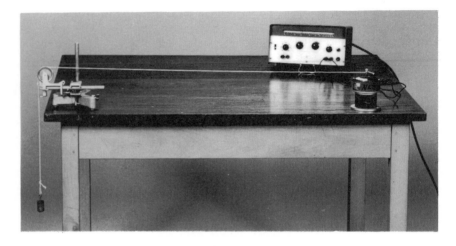

Figure 2.19

A stationary wave pattern

1 Attach a string, of uniform thickness and length approximately 150 cm, to one end of the vibrator, mounted so that its movement is vertical. Pass the other end of the string over a small pulley and attach a mass (e.g. 100 g) as shown in figure 2.19.

2 Connect the vibrator to the signal generator. Observe the amplitude of the string's transverse motion as the frequency is slowly increased and then decreased.

3 Find the lowest frequency that produces a point of maximum displacement at the mid-point of the string (i.e. one loop in the string). Record this frequency.

Note. You may need to adjust the tension in the string and/or the length of the string to obtain this pattern.

4 Keep the tension and length constant and find the lowest frequency that produces a stationary point at the midpoint of the string (i.e. two loops). Record this frequency.

5 Find a relationship between the number of loops n and frequency f, for the same values of T and l.

Relationship between T and f

1 Adjust the frequency to produce a pattern as shown in figure 2.20. Record the values of the tension T and frequency f.

2 Increase the tension (by adding an additional mass) and find the new frequency at which the string has the same mode of vibration. Record the values of T and f.

3 Repeat step 2 for at least three other values of tension.

4 Plot graphs which show the relationship between frequency and tension. Write down an equation which relates these quantities.

(*Hint.* It is difficult to interpret a curve but a straight line will indicate a relation more conclusively.)

Figure 2.20

EXPERIMENT WV 7

Vibrations in an air column

Apparatus

○ signal generator
○ loudspeaker, diameter 60 mm
○ resonance tube
○ metre rule
○ cardboard tube, length 25 cm

Modes of vibration

1 Set up the apparatus as shown in figure 2.21. The rate of flow of water from a tap and out to a sink can be varied so that the level of water in the tube can be made to rise and fall slowly or rapidly, or remain at the same level.

2 Fix the water level so that the length of the air column is about 25 cm.

3 Switch on the signal generator and set the frequency at about 50 Hz. Adjust the output control so that the note can just be heard.

4 Gradually increase the frequency until there is a sharp increase in volume. Record this frequency f_1.

5 Continue to increase the frequency until there is a second further increase in volume. Record this frequency f_2.

6 Repeat step 5 and record a third frequency f_3.

7 Explain your observations using the terms fundamental frequency, resonance, harmonic, overtone. What is the relationship between f_1 and f_2, and between f_1 and f_3?

8 Repeat steps 3, 4, 5 and 6 for an open pipe (e.g. a cardboard tube of fixed length 25 cm) and comment on your observations.

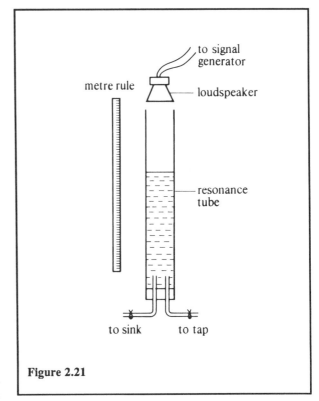

Figure 2.21

continued

EXPERIMENT WV 7

Speed of sound in air

1 Set the frequency at a fixed value of 1000 Hz. Record the frequency f.

2 Bring the water gradually to the top of the tube. (Take care, in order to prevent the water flowing over the sides of the tube!)

3 Allow the water level to fall slowly until a sharp increase in the loudness of the sound (resonance) is heard. Make minor adjustments in order to obtain the position of maximum loudness. Measure the length of the air column, repeat the procedure several times and then find the mean value l_1.

4 Now find the second position of resonance, using the same frequency (the air column will be about three times the length). Obtain a mean value l_2, for the length of the air column at which resonance occurs.

5 The diagrams in figure 2.22 represent the vibrations of the air column in the first and second positions of resonance. Show that the speed of sound c in air is given by $c = 2f(l_2 - l_1)$. Use your results to calculate a value for the speed of sound in air.

6 Repeat steps 2 and 3 with at least four other lower frequencies. Find a mean value of the length l of the resonating air column in each case.

7 Plot a graph of l (y-axis) against $1/f$ (x-axis).

8 Use your graph to find (i) a mean value for the speed of sound in air at this temperature, and (ii) the end-correction of the pipe.

9 Measure the diameter of the pipe. Calculate the ratio of the end correction to the diameter of the pipe.

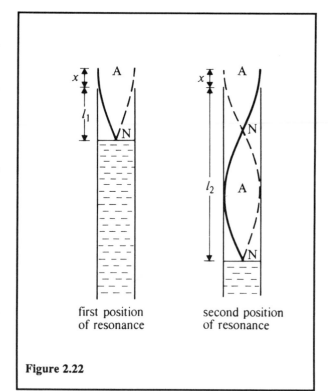

first position   second position
of resonance   of resonance

Figure 2.22

Questions on objectives

1 Figure 2.23 represents a longitudinal progressive wave. Which of the distances marked (A-E) is
(a) the amplitude of the wave,
(b) the wavelength of the wave? *(objective 3)*

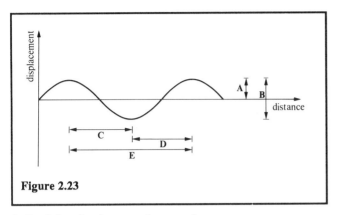

Figure 2.23

2 Explain what is meant by a stationary wave.
A stationary sinusoidal transverse wave is set up in a string so that there are nodes at the ends and mid-point only. The displacement of each point on the string is a maximum when $t = 0$. Draw, on the same diagram, the positions of the string at $t = 0, t = T/8, t = 4, t = 3T/8, t = T/2$, where T is the period. *(objectives 1, 4 and 13)*

3 The apparatus illustrated in figure 2.24 shows a possible method of measuring the speed of sound in air. Sound from a loudspeaker is passed through a system of tubing, and reaches a detector by two paths, A and B. The length of path B can be varied by moving the sliding tube.

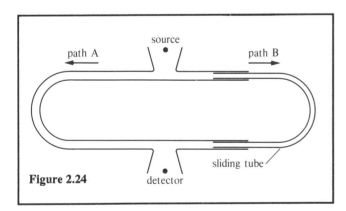

Figure 2.24

(a) When the sliding tube is moved, the intensity of the sound varies from a minimum to a maximum, to a minimum again, and so on. Explain this.
(b) In a particular experiment the tube was moved a distance of 68 mm between successive minima of sound. The frequency of the source was 2500 Hz. Calculate a value for the speed of sound. (objective 7 and 8)

4 Two loudspeakers X and Y are connected in parallel to an audio-frequency oscillator (signal generator). An observer at a point O, which is equidistant from X and Y, detects a sound of maximum intensity. As the observer moves parallel to XY the intensity decreases, and first falls to a minimum at a point P. The distances PX and PY are measured and found to be 0.50 m and 0.35 m respectively.

(a) Calculate the wavelength of the sound waves.
(b) Calculate the speed of sound in air if the frequency of the source is 1.14 Hz. *(objective 8)*

5 When two musical notes of slightly different frequencies are sounded together, a listener is aware of a kind of throbbing: a periodic rise and fall in the loudness of the sound.
(a) What name is given to this phenomenon?
(b) Explain this observation qualitatively, in terms of the principle of superposition of waves. *(objective 9)*

6 An accurately calibrated tuning fork of frequency 320 Hz is sounded with the note D of a piano and a beat frequency of 2 Hz is heard. What are the possible frequencies of the piano string? *(objective 9)*

7 A police car travelling at a speed of 34 m s^{-1} passes a stationary observer. The police car siren emits a note of frequency 450 Hz. Calculate the apparent change in frequency of the note as the police car approaches the observer and passes him. The speed of sound in air is 340 m s^{-1}. *(objective 11)*

8 Describe and explain, with the aid of a suitable diagram, the motion of the air in a tube open at both ends and vibrating in its fundamental mode. *(objective 14)*

9 Compare the properties of a stationary wave pattern in air with those of a progressive sound wave in respect of (i) amplitude, (ii) pressure variation, (iii) phase. *(objective 6)*

10 The speed of a transverse wave along a string is given by $c = \sqrt{\dfrac{T}{\mu}}$ where T is the tension and μ the mass per unit length.

(a) Explain how reflection may give rise to transverse stationary waves in a stretched string of length l.
(b) Use the above expression for the speed to derive the frequency f of the fundamental mode of vibration. *(objectives 5 and 13)*

11 In a resonance tube experiment, series of results for the minimum length l of the air column in a resonance tube closed at one end, resonating to a loudspeaker at various frequencies f, were obtained. A graph is plotted of l (y-axis) against $1/f$ (x-axis).
(a) Sketch the graph you would expect to obtain.
(b) How would you obtain a value for the speed of sound in an air column from the graph?
(c) What is the significance of the intercept on the l axis ($1/f = 0$)? *(objective 15)*

12 A loudspeaker is connected to a signal generator and placed several metres from a smooth wall. The signal generator is switched on and the frequency is adjusted to 6.0×10^2 Hz.
(a) Assuming that the loudspeaker is positioned so that waves are incident normally on the wall, what happens to the soundwaves at the wall?
(b) Assuming no energy loss at the wall, explain what happens

to the air molecules in a region up to 1.5 m from the wall. *(objective 4 and 5)*

13 A steel wire of diameter 0.50 mm is clamped tightly between two supports 20 cm apart under a tension of 100 N. Find the frequency of the lowest note that the string emits when it is plucked.

(Density of steel = 7.9×10^3 kg m^{-3}.) *(objective 16)*

TOPIC 3
Optics

Summary

A debate about the nature of light opens this topic. The major part of the topic uses a ray treatment of light to describe phenomena and explain the operation of optical instruments. How does a ray fit into the wave model (or particle model) of light?

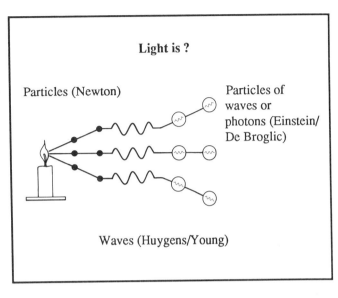

Light is ?

Particles (Newton)

Particles of waves or photons (Einstein/ De Broglic)

Waves (Huygens/Young)

Objectives

When you have completed the work in this chapter, you should be able to:

1 Use the following scientific terms correctly: critical angle, total internal reflection, apparent depth, minimum deviation, refracting angle of a prism, focal plane, virtual object, power of a lens.

2 Define the following scientific terms: refractive index, principal axis, optical centre, principal focus, focal length, linear magnification, normal adjustment of a telescope, eye-ring, angular magnification (magnifying power).

3 Explain what is meant by total internal reflection and critical angle and give practical applications of each.

4 State the laws of refraction.

5 Recall and use the relationship between refractive index, real depth and apparent depth (for normal incidence).

6 State the significance of a sign convention and use the 'real is positive' sign convention correctly in calculations.

7 Describe experiments to determine the focal length of thin lenses and spherical mirrors.

8 Describe the optical system and action of a refracting astronomical telescope in normal adjustment, including diagrams of the paths of rays of light through the telescope from a distant non-axial point.

9 Describe the optical system and action of a compound microscope, and draw diagrams of the paths of rays from a non-axial point which produce an image at the near point.

10 Solve problems involving use of refractive index, the lens formula $\frac{1}{f} = \frac{1}{u} + \frac{1}{v}$ and linear magnification.

11 State Huygens' hypothesis. Explain how it is used in constructing reflected and refracted wavefronts, and show how this construction is in agreement with the laws of reflection and refraction.

Experiments

WV 8	The converging lens	(1 hour)
WV 9	The astronomical telescope	(0.75 hour)

References

Akrill	Chapters 25 and 26
Bolton	Chapter 9
Duncan	Chapter 6
Muncaster	Chapters 18-23
Nelkon	Chapters 14, 15, 16 and 18
Whelan	Chapters 31, 32, 33 and 36

3.1 Light - wave or particle?

What is light? What is vision? It is hard for us to realise that in the days of ancient Greece, and even much later, the question debated was whether we see because something enters our eyes from objects (Aristotle's view) or whether our eyes send out a stream of something which collides with an object to make it visible (Plato's view). It was only at the beginning of the seventeenth century that light was accepted as something emitted by luminous objects. The great debate was then about the nature of this emission. Two theories of light were proposed: the corpuscular theory of Newton and the wave theory of Huygens. In the following two sections we consider the way in which these theories attempted to provide explanations about the behaviour of light.

Newton's corpuscles

In his famous book 'Opticks', published in 1704, Isaac Newton proposed that light rays were streams of very small bodies (corpuscles) emitted from shining substances. He could not support the idea that light was waves, because he observed that light clearly travels in straight lines and produces sharp shadows: '...*waves on the surface of still water passing by the sides of a broad obstacle which stops part of them bend afterwards and spread gradually into the quiet water behind the obstacle. The waves ..., wherein sounds consist, bend manifestly though not so much as the waves of water.... Light is never known to follow crooked passages nor to bend into the shadow...*'

Newton did not merely propose a theory but produced much experimental evidence, much of it never reported before and, in each case, his theory was offered as an explanation. These experiments included his investigation of the dispersion of white light into a spectrum and interference effects in thin films (Newton's rings). The way light was reflected suggested to Newton an elastic collision between corpuscles and the reflecting medium. Refraction, he explained as follows: that bodies refract light by acting upon its rays in lines perpendicular to their surface. He concluded that at a refracting boundary the motion (speed or momentum) perpendicular to the boundary would be altered whilst the motion of the ray parallel to the boundary would be unchanged.

Newton studied the concentric dark and bright rings formed when light was reflected or transmitted in a thin film of air between a curved lens surface and a flat glass surface. He even observed diffraction effects due to a hair, but though he observed diffraction fringes and a broadening of the shadow, every observation was explained to his own satisfaction in terms of the interaction between the corpuscles of light and matter.

Huygens' wavelets

Christiaan Huygens published his 'Treatise on light' in 1690. In this he proposed that light: '...*spreads, as sound does, by spherical surfaces and waves: for I will call them waves from their resemblance to those which are seen to be formed in water when a stone is thrown into it...*'

One of his main arguments was that rays of light are observed to pass through each other. He could not imagine streams of particles doing this, but he did believe that waves could because this happened also with sound waves. Huygens was impressed by the similarities between sound and light, and found it necessary to introduce the idea of a medium ('ethereal matter') between earth and sun to transmit light waves. He explored the idea of light being similar to water waves, to explain both reflection and refraction.

One of the strongest reasons why Newton rejected the wave theory was his belief that waves required a medium in which to travel, and light seemed to travel through space without a medium. Newton made a unique contribution to the study of the nature of light, by providing a lot of new experimental evidence, and he identified the key questions even though many of his answers were rejected by later scientists in favour of an explanation in terms of a wave model.

One key question was the possibility of interaction between light and matter, a factor neglected by many scientists in the eighteenth and nineteenth centuries. Twentieth century studies of such interactions have led to the development of a wave-particle theory of light.

Q 3.1 Discussion question

What are the strengths and weaknesses of these opposing theories? What do you know of the **photon** - is it a wave or a particle? ∎

In this unit we will be studying light as a wave. Though some of its wave properties are less apparent than those of mechanical waves, we will see that light shows all the behaviour of a transverse wave described in topic 1. The nature of the photon will be considered in the unit *Electrons and the nucleus*.

3.2 Huygens' construction

Huygens' hypothesis states that every point on an existing wavefront can be considered as a source of secondary wavelets which radiate out with the wave velocity.

Huygens' construction applies this statement as follows: from a given position of the wavefront, a later position can be constructed by drawing the envelope of all the secondary wavelets (figure 3.1). The effect produced at some point ahead of the wave (the amplitude of the disturbance) must be the result of superposing (adding up the amplitudes of) all the secondary wavelets.

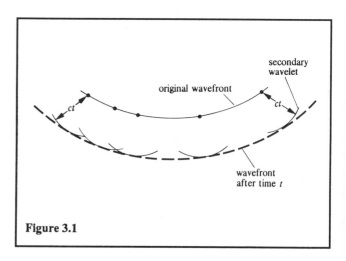

Figure 3.1

Reflection

Q 3.2 Study question

In figure 3.2, AB is a wavefront approaching a reflecting surface at speed c. The angle of incidence is i. A secondary wavelet from B travels to B_1 in time t.

(a) Sketch the diagram and use Huygens' construction to determine the position of the reflected wavefront after time t. Show that the angles of incidence and reflection are equal.

(b) Sketch the wavefront a time $2t/3$ after it has left the position AB. ■

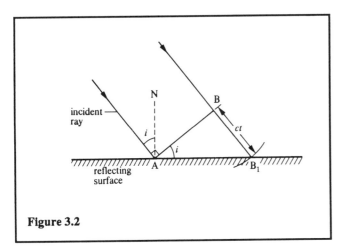

incident ray

N

B

ct

i

i

A

B_1

reflecting surface

Figure 3.2

Refraction

Q 3.3 Study question

In figure 3.3, AB is a wavefront approaching a boundary between two media with a wave speed c_1. The angle of incidence is i_1. The wavespeed is c_2 in the second medium.

Sketch the diagram and, assuming that $c_2 = 2c_1/3$, construct the refracted wavefront A_1B_1. If this is at an angle i_2 with the boundary, show that

$$\frac{c_1}{c_2} = \frac{\sin i_1}{\sin i_2} \qquad ■$$

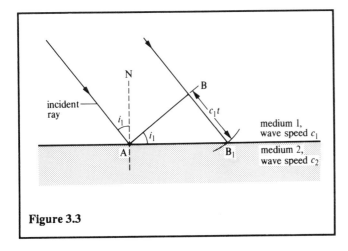

incident ray

N

B

c_1t

i_1

i_1

A

B_1

medium 1, wave speed c_1

medium 2, wave speed c_2

Figure 3.3

Snell's law of refraction, formulated from experiments in 1626, holds for light and for other wave motions. It states that, for waves of a given frequency,

$$\frac{\sin i_2}{\sin i_1} = \text{a constant, for two given media.}$$

Wave theory shows that this constant is the ratio of the wave speeds in the two media (c_1/c_2). This ratio is called the **refractive index** for waves travelling from medium 1 into medium 2.

The refractive index $_1n_2$ for waves passing from medium 1 to medium 2 is defined as:

$$_1n_2 = \frac{\text{speed of light in medium 1}}{\text{speed of light in medium 2}} = \frac{c_1}{c_2} \qquad (1)$$

The number of waves per second crossing the boundary is the same for both media, i.e. the frequency f is constant.

$$f = \frac{c}{\lambda}$$

When the speed changes, there must be a corresponding change in wavelength.

From equation (1) this gives

$$_1n_2 = \frac{c_1}{c_2} = \frac{\lambda_1}{\lambda_2}$$

This change in speed or wavelength by different media will produce a dispersion of the colours in white light, when it passes through glass for example. The refractive index of blue light is different from that of red light.

3.3 Light as rays

The wavelength of light is less than a millionth of a metre. Because of this, diffraction effects due to light waves occur on a very small scale and are difficult to observe, except in a few cases when the light waves are restricted by tiny apertures. This is why our common experience persuades us that light is not diffracted round corners but travels in straight lines.

In this topic we shall *not* consider waves restricted by tiny apertures or obstacles and so we shall ignore diffraction effects and consider the behaviour of light in terms of **rays**. This is defined as a normal to the wavefront, and also as a line which indicates the direction in which the wave energy is travelling.

You may have studied the behaviour of light by observing very narrow beams or 'ray streaks'. We can observe beams when they strike a reflecting surface or when light in the beam is scattered as it travels through dust or smoke particles. When a source produces a beam of light, the wave energy is concentrated within a limited cross-section. The path of the light energy - a ray - can be traced by observing the behaviour of very narrow beams. Even the narrowest beam, however, has a finite width. There is no such thing as a single ray. Nevertheless, the ray concept is very useful in describing the behaviour of light waves, just as lines (defined as having no thickness) are very useful in geometry even though we can never draw them. The behaviour of light waves, when they strike mirrors, lenses or prisms, is conveniently described by rays. **Geometrical optics** is the name given to the study of light in terms of rays. As this name implies, it is possible to describe much of what is observed in terms of simple geometry and a few basic laws.

Laws of reflection and refraction

For example, you will no doubt have observed a situation similar to that shown in figure 3.4.

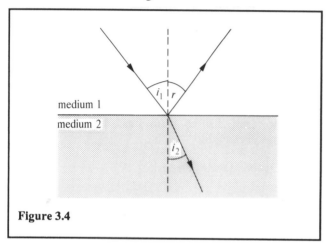

Figure 3.4

Q 3.4 Study question

State the laws which apply to the reflection and the refraction illustrated in figure 3.4. ■

Q 3.5 Self-assessment question

Why is it necessary to define refractive index for a specific colour of light? ■

Q 3.6 Self-assessment question

(a) Will a ray of light be refracted towards or away from the normal when travelling from glass to water? Explain. (Refractive index of water = 1.33, refractive index of glass = 1.50.)
(b) A ray of light travelling in glass strikes a plane glass-water interface at an angle of incidence of 50°. Calculate the angle of refraction in the water. ■

Real and apparent depth

When viewed from above the surface, a pool of water appears to be less deep than it really is, because rays of light from a point O (figure 3.5a) are refracted away from the normal at the water-air interface and appear to come from point I. This is the image position for normal viewing. In figure 3.5b the same object O, viewed obliquely, will appear to be at I_1. As the viewing position becomes more oblique, the image moves along the path shown, getting nearer to the surface.

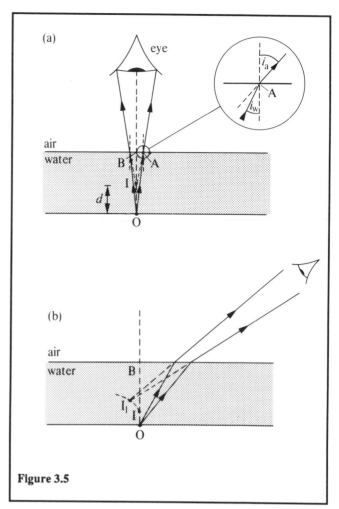

Figure 3.5

Q 3.7 Development question

In figure 3.5a, for refraction at point A from water to air,

$$_a n_w = \frac{\sin i_a}{\sin i_w}$$

Show that for normal viewing, when i_w and i_a are both small angles,

$$_a n_w = \frac{\sin i_a}{\sin i_w} = \frac{OB}{IB} = \frac{\text{real depth}}{\text{apparent depth}} \qquad ■$$

Q 3.8 Self-assessment question

A travelling microscope is focused on a scratch on the bottom of a beaker. Turpentine is poured into the beaker to a depth of 4.00 cm, and the microcope is raised through a vertical distance of 1.30 cm to bring the scratch into focus again. Calculate the refractive index of turpentine. ■

Total internal reflection and critical angle

If a ray of light is travelling from one medium to an optically less dense medium (for example, from glass to air) with an angle of incidence of about 30°, it is refracted away from the normal. Part of the incident light is also reflected.

Q 3.9 Self-assessment question

(a) What happens to the angle of refraction as the angle of incidence is gradually increased?
(b) What is the maximum value of the angle of refraction? ■

The name given to the limiting value of the angle of incidence, for which the refracted ray just emerges along the boundary between the two media, is the **critical angle**, c (figure 3.6). If the angle of incidence is increased beyond the critical angle, the reflected ray becomes suddenly brighter and no refracted ray is observed. All the incident light is being reflected, and **total internal reflection** occurs. ■

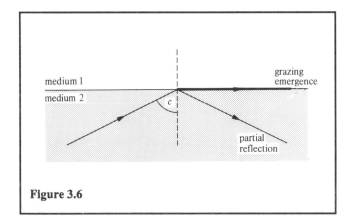

Figure 3.6

Q 3.10 Self-assessment question

(a) By applying Snell's law to the critical ray, show that

$$_1n_2 = 1/\sin c$$

(b) Calculate the a critical angle for an air-glass boundary, if the refractive index of the glass is 1.50.
(c) What are the two conditions that must be satisfied in order for total internal reflection to occur?
(d) What do you find if you try to calculate the angle of refraction for an angle of incidence greater than the critical angle? How does the mathematical result correspond to physical observation? ■

Q 3.11 Study question

Explain, with the aid of diagrams, how a right-angled isosceles prism can be used to deviate a ray of light through (i) 90° and (ii) 180°. ■

Q 3.12 Self-assessment question

In figure 3.7, ABCD is a plan view of a glass cube. A horizontal beam of light enters the face AB at grazing incidence.
(a) Show that the emergent angle θ for rays emerging from AD is given by sin θ = 1/tan c, where c is the critical angle.
(b) What is the greatest value for the refractive index of glass if any of the light is to emerge from AD?
(c) If the glass has a greater refractive index than this, where will the light emerge? ■

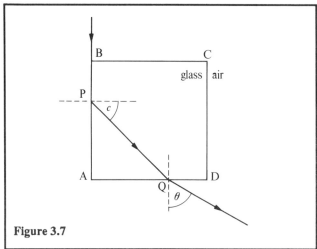

Figure 3.7

Because of the phenomenon of total internal reflection, it is possible to 'pipe' light along a bent transparent rod, provided that the curvature of the rod is not too great. A beam of light entering one end of the rod is totally internally reflected when it meets a wall, and is trapped within the rod, eventually emerging from the other end with little loss of intensity. Very thin transparent fibres behave in the same way, and the study of their properties and applications is an active field of research and development known as **fibre optics**. Devices using bundles of optical fibres have a wide range of applications. In medical science, for example, light pipes can be used for examining the interior of the lungs. In telecommunications, they can be used for the transmission of pulses of light which can carry large quantities of information (figure 3.8).

Figure 3.8

Q 3.13 Discussion question

What do you think are the advantages of optical fibres in transmitting telephonic information, compared to the conventional method of passing electrical signals down cables? ■

There is a further study of the uses of optical fibres in the Topic Options 'Medical Physics' and 'Telecommunications' in the *Student's resource book*.

Prisms

A prism is a block of material (usually glass) with a triangular cross-section (figure 3.9a).

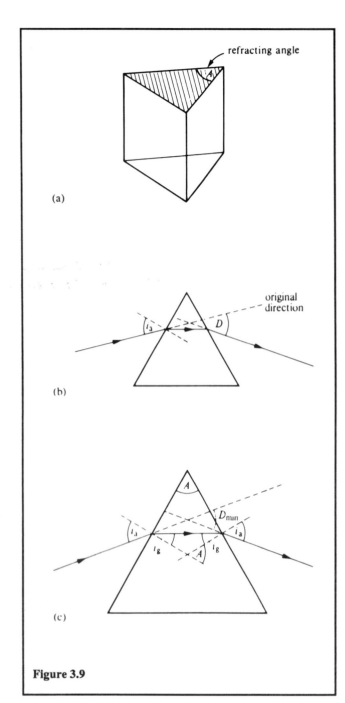

(a)

(b)

original direction

(c)

Figure 3.9

It is used in optical instruments to produce a change in direction (**deviation**) of beams of light which pass through it. This is because the deviation by refraction at the first surface is not cancelled by the second, as it would be in a parallel sided block (figure 3.9b).

If white light is passed through a prism, each colour will be deviated by a different amount, because of the change in speed of each colour. This results in **dispersion** and the production of a **spectrum**, as in Newton's classic experiment. This property of a prism is used in a spectrometer, which is an instrument for analysing the nature of a source of light (see topic 5).

The angle between the original (incident) direction of light and the final (refracted) direction is called the angle of deviation, D. D depends on the angle of incidence, i. When the ray of light passes symmetrically through the prism (figure 3.9c) D is a minimum.

Q 3.14 Study question

Show that the angle of minimum deviation D_{min} of a prism is

$$D_{min} = 2i - A \qquad \blacksquare$$

3.4 Thin lenses

There are many different shapes of lens, but all lenses can be classified as either converging or diverging. We shall restrict our study to thin lenses, for which the diameter of the lens is large compared to its maximum thickness.

Q 3.15 Study question

Define the following terms as applied to a converging lens and a diverging lens: principal axis, optical centre C, principal focus F, focal length f, and focal plane. ■

Images in lenses

Information about the position and nature of the image formed by a lens can be obtained either by drawing a ray diagram or by calculation. Both methods are shown in the worked example in figure 3.10 which also summarises the 'real is positive' sign convention and some lens formulae. In lens calculations using these formulae, only small objects on the principal axis are considered. All rays are, therefore, **paraxial** (close to the principal axis and making small angles with it).

Q 3.16 Self-assessment question

(a) A converging lens of focal length 15 cm forms a virtual image 20 cm from the lens. What values would you substitute in the lens formula to calculate the object distance?
(b) An object is placed 10 cm from a diverging lens of focal length 20 cm. What values would you substitute in the lens formula to calculate the image distance? ■

Q 3.17 Self-assessment question

(a) An object is placed 10 cm from a converging lens of focal length 20 cm. Calculate the position, nature and magnification of the image.
(b) What is the nature of the image formed by a diverging lens of a real object? Sketch a ray diagram to show how it is formed.
(c) An erect image, 2 cm high, is formed 10 cm from a diverging lens of focal length 15 cm. Calculate the position and size of the object. ■

Q 3.18 Self-assessment question

Two thin lenses are placed coaxially 15 cm apart. A beam of light parallel to the axis strikes the first lens, which is a converging lens of focal length 20 cm. The second lens is a diverging lens, also of focal length 20 cm.

(a) Sketch the paths of two rays of light through the optical system and show the position of the final image.
(b) Calculate the position of the final image using the lens formula. Is it a real or a virtual image? ■

'Real is positive' sign convention

Positive

Distances actually traversed by rays, i.e. distance between **real** objects or images and the optical centre of a lens (or mirror).

Focal length of **converging** lens.

Radius of curvature of lens surface if **convex** to the less dense medium.

Focal length and radius of curvature of a **concave** mirror.

Negative

Distances apparently traversed by rays, i.e. distances between **virtual** objects or images and the optical centre of a lens (or mirror).

Focal length of **diverging** lens.

Radius of curvature of lens surface if **concave** to the less dense medium.

Focal length and radius of curvature of a **convex** mirror.

Lens formula

$$\frac{1}{f} = \frac{1}{u} + \frac{1}{v}$$

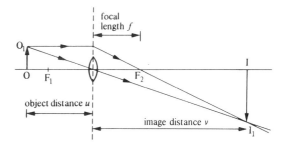

Linear magnification m

$$m = \frac{\text{image height (or width)}}{\text{object height (or width)}}$$

$$m = \frac{II_1}{OO_1} = \frac{v}{u}$$

Power of a lens

$$\frac{\text{power}}{\text{[dioptres]}} = \frac{1}{\text{focal length [metres]}}$$

$$F = \frac{1}{f}$$

Figure 3.10

Worked example

Question

An object is placed 30 cm from a converging lens A of focal length 20 cm. Another converging lens B, of focal length 40 cm, is placed coaxially with A and 20 cm from it on the side away from the object. Find the position, nature and magnification of the image formed by the two lenses.

Calculations

For lens A, f = +20 cm, u = +30 cm.

$$\frac{1}{+20 \text{ cm}} = \frac{1}{+30 \text{ cm}} + \frac{1}{v}$$

$$\frac{1}{v} = \frac{1}{+20 \text{ cm}} - \frac{1}{+30 \text{ cm}}$$

$$\frac{1}{v} = \frac{1}{+60 \text{ cm}}$$

$$v = +60 \text{ cm}$$

Magnification produced by lens A = 60/30 = 2.

The light is intercepted by lens B 20 cm from lens A. The image formed by lens A acts as a virtual object for lens B.

For lens B, f = +40 cm, u = -40 cm.

$$\frac{1}{+40 \text{ cm}} = \frac{1}{-40 \text{ cm}} + \frac{1}{v}$$

$$\frac{1}{v} = \frac{1}{+40 \text{ cm}} - \frac{1}{-40 \text{ cm}}$$

$$\frac{1}{v} = \frac{2}{+40 \text{ cm}}$$

$$v = +20 \text{ cm}$$

Magnification produced by lens B = 20/40 = 1/2
Total magnification = 2 x 1/2 = 1.
The final image is 20 cm from B, on the side away from A, real, and the same size as the object.

Ray diagram

Real rays are shown by solid lines, virtual rays by broken lines.

Lenses or mirrors are represented by straight broken lines, with a small lens or mirror drawn in the middle to indicate the type used.

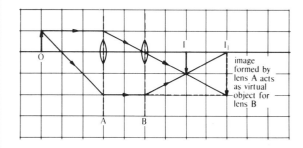

image formed by lens A acts as virtual object for lens B

Measuring focal length

A thin converging lens forms a real image of an object placed further away from the lens than the principal focus. The position of the image and its size (if necessary) can be found by experiment, and the focal length of the lens can be determined by a suitable graphical method. The following is a brief summary of the methods available for finding the focal length of a converging lens.

1 Measure u and v, and draw a graph of $1/u$ against $1/v$ or of u against v.

2 Place a plane mirror behind the lens and locate the point where the object and image coincide.

3 Measure m and v, and find f from the relationship $v/f = m + 1$.

E Experiment WV 8
The converging lens

This experiment is included to give you some practical experience of handling lenses and to help you gain familiarity with two standard methods, if you have not carried these out earlier in your study of physics.

A diverging lens cannot produce a real image if a diverging beam from a real object is incident at the lens. However, if the light from the object is made to converge sufficiently, by a converging lens, before it meets the diverging lens, a real image can be produced. The image which the converging beam would form, but for the diverging lens, is a **virtual object** whose distance u, from the diverging lens, has a negative value.

Q 3.19 Study question

Make brief notes on how you would determine the focal length of a diverging lens by using a converging lens. ∎

3.5 Spherical mirrors

Spherical mirrors reflect light so that a parallel beam can be made convergent (by a concave mirror) or divergent (by a convex mirror). A concave mirror can perform a similar task to a converging lens. For example, telescopes can be constructed using either a converging lens or a concave mirror. This brief study of the optical properties of mirrors is confined mainly to mirrors of small aperture, that is, mirrors for which the diameter (distance across) is small compared to the radius of curvature. When large aperture mirrors are required (for example, for headlamp reflectors) they are usually made parabolic, not spherical, because a large aperture spherical mirror has no precise focus and does not produce clear images.

Q 3.20 Study question

Define the focal length of a spherical mirror, using and explaining the terms 'paraxial rays' and 'principal focus'. ∎

Q 3.21 Study question

Show that for a spherical mirror the focal length is approximately equal to half its radius of curvature, indicating the approximations which are applicable. ∎

Images in mirrors

The geometry of image formation is similar to that for thin lenses (see figure 3.10) except that rays are reflected back from the mirror instead of refracted through the lens. For paraxial rays incident at a spherical mirror of small aperture,

$$\frac{2}{r} = \frac{1}{f} = \frac{1}{u} + \frac{1}{v}$$

where r is the radius of curvature, u the object distance and v the image distance. This formula is applicable to all spherical mirrors for objects at any distance from the mirror, provided the sign convention ('real is positive') is applied. On this convention the focal length of a concave mirror is positive.

Q 3.22 Study question

Draw a ray diagram to show how a convex mirror forms a virtual, erect, diminished image. ∎

Q 3.23 Self-assessment question

A concave mirror forms an erect image 45 cm from the object and four times its height.

(a) Where must the mirror be situated?
(b) What is its radius of curvature?
(c) Through what distance must the object be moved to form an inverted image of the same magnification? ∎

Measurement of focal length

The focal length of a concave mirror can be found by the following methods.

1 Adjusting the position of an object until it coincides with its own image (the self-conjugate or no-parallax method).

2 Obtaining several values for object and image distances and finding f from a graph of $1/u$ against $1/v$.

Q 3.24 Study question

Make brief notes on the above methods of measuring the focal length of a concave mirror. ∎

3.6 Optical instruments

An optical instrument is used to extend the limits of perception of the human eye. When an object is placed inside the principal focus of a converging lens, it forms a magnified image. This is a simple form of microscope. When we considered the magnification produced by a lens we introduced the idea of linear magnification m. In some optical instruments the final image is formed at infinity. In such a case m would be infinite! The linear magnification is, therefore, not a very helpful indication of the improvement produced by the optical instrument.

The apparent size of an object depends upon the size of its image formed on the retina of the eye. This depends upon the angle which is subtended at the eye (the visual angle).

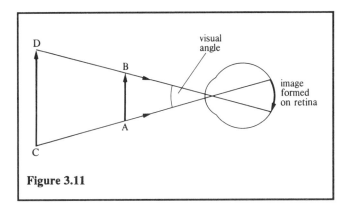

Figure 3.11

In figure 3.11 the image sizes of the two objects AB and CD will appear to be the same.

Q 3.25 Self-assessment question

Explain why the two cars shown in figure 3.12 appear to be the same size in figure 3.12a. ▪

Figure 3.12

The eye has the ability to **accommodate** (i.e. to change the converging power of the lens system), so that it can see clearly objects situated over a wide, but limited, range of distances. The rays emerging from an optical instrument must, therefore, appear to come from an image in this region of clear vision.

Q 3.26 Study question

What is meant by the terms *accommodation, near point, far point* and *least distance of distinct vision*? ▪

Angular magnification

Telescopes and microscopes are instruments designed to produce an image which subtends a greater angle at the eye than the original object does. They make objects look bigger by producing a bigger image on the retina of the eye.

The angular magnification *M* (or **magnifying power**) of an optical instrument is defined by the equation

$$M = \frac{\beta}{\alpha}$$

where ß is the angle subtended at the eye by the final image formed by the instrument, and α is the angle subtended at the eye by the object, at some specified distance, without the use of the instrument.

Telescopes view distant fixed objects, so for telescopes α is the angle subtended at the unaided eye by the fixed distant object.

When examining small objects with the unaided eye, the best we can do is bring them as close as possible to the eye, to the near point. So, for microscopes, the angle α is the angle subtended by the object when placed at the least distance of distinct vision.

Q 3.27 Self-assessment question

(a) What is the distinction between angular magnification *M* and linear magnification *m*?
(b) Write down an equation defining the angular magnification of a microscope. ▪

Magnifying glass

Q 3.28 Study question

(a) Describe, with the aid of a ray diagram, how a converging lens can be used as a magnifying glass so that the final image is at the near point (i.e. the instrument is in normal adjustment).
(b) Where must the object be placed so that the final image is at infinity? ▪

Q 3.29 Development question

An expression for the angular magnification *M* of a magnifying glass can be derived in terms of the focal length *f* and the least distance of distinct vision *D*. Figure 3.13 shows a magnifying glass producing an image at the near point, viewed by an eye very close to the lens.
(a) Calculate the object distance *u* in terms of *f* and *D*.
(b) Hence show that the angular magnification *M* is given by $M = (D/f) + 1$ (assuming angles α and ß are small, so that tan ß = ß, etc.).
(c) Show that when the final image is at infinity the magnifying power is given by $M = D/f$. ▪

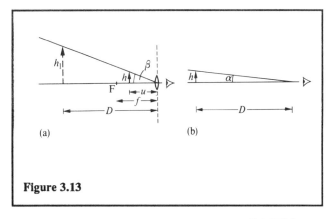

Figure 3.13

Q 3.30 Self-assessment question

(a) What is the focal length of the lens which can be used as a magnifying glass in normal adjustment with a magnifying power of 6?

(b) Using this lens, the image is located 300 mm from the eye. Calculate the object position and hence deduce the angular magnification produced in this case.

(c) Where must the final image be located to produce (i) maximum angular magnification, and (ii) minimum angular magnification? ■

Astronomical telescope

A refracting astronomical telescope is constructed using two converging lenses, a long focal length objective and a shorter focal length eyepiece.

Q 3.31 Development question*

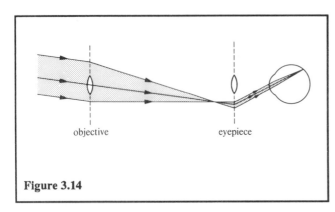

objective   eyepiece

Figure 3.14

Figure 3.14 shows a beam of light which originated at one point; the top of a distant object. After passing through the telescope, the light is focused at a point on the retina of the observer's eye.

(a) What is located at the point between the lenses where the light converges? What is the distance from the objective lens to this point?

(b) What kind of image is the eye looking at, and where is it located?

(c) What kind of image is produced on the retina?

(d) What is the distance between the lenses of the telescope shown in figure 3.14? ■

The telescope objective produces a real inverted image which acts as an object for the second lens. This is used as a simple magnifying glass, producing a virtual inverted image between the near and far points of the observer's eye. In normal adjustment the final image is located at infinity, as this is most comfortable for the eye.

Figure 3.15 shows one ray from the top of a distant object, which passes through the optical centre of the objective and is refracted through the second lens. The position and size of image I_1, formed by the objective, is shown. How do we find the correct path for a ray from this image to the eye? If the final image is located at infinity, all the rays leaving the eyepiece will be parallel. The construction line through the centre of the eyepiece is one path which a ray could take through the lens without refraction, and if the image is at infinity all the rays emerging from the lens must be parallel to this construction line. We can use this diagram to find the magnifying power of the telescope.

Q 3.32 Development question

(a) Why is the angle α (figure 3.15) the same as the angle subtended at the unaided eye by the object?

(b) Express α in terms of h_1 and f_o and ß in terms of h_1 and f_e.

(c) Show that angular magnification $= f_o/f_e$, for normal adjustment.

(d) If the final image is at a finite distance the magnification will be f_o/u, where u is the distance from the image I_1 to the eyepiece. Is the magnifying power greater or less than f_o/f_e in this case? Explain why.

(e) Suggest possible specifications for the lenses to be used in constructing a portable astronomical telescope of magnifying power 50. ■

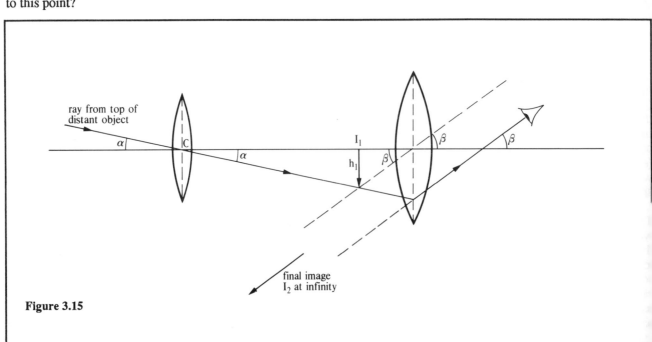

ray from top of distant object

final image I_2 at infinity

Figure 3.15

Q 3.33 Self-assessment question

An astronomical telescope consists of two thin converging lenses of focal lengths 100 cm and 5 cm. It is used for viewing a distant object.

a) Calculate the angular magnification when it is used in normal adjustment.
b) The telescope is adjusted so that the final image is at the near point, 25 cm from the eyepiece. Calculate the distance of the intermediate image from the eyepiece.
c) What is the angular magnification when it is used in near point adjustment? ■

Experiment WV 9
The astronomical telescope

In this experiment you will construct a simple telescope, and measure the angular magnification it produces.

Now try drawing the paths of rays through a telescope to help to explain how it works. The purpose of such a ray diagram is not to locate exact image positions for particular lenses, but to show the general principle for all such instruments, so the exact positions of the focal points will not be included. Any appropriate positions can be chosen for the object and images but the images must be drawn to the correct sizes for their particular positions.

Q 3.34 Study question

Draw a ray diagram to show the paths of rays from two non-axial points (e.g. the top and bottom of an object) through an astronomical telescope in normal adjustment, following the instructions below.

a) Draw a diagram like figure 3.15 showing the path of one ray accurately.
b) Draw the paths of two more rays from the top of the object passing through the top and bottom of the objective (distinguish clearly between actual rays and construction lines).
c) Suppose the object lies across the axis, with the axis through its midpoint. Draw three more rays, from the bottom of the object, making an angle α with the axis (first draw an image I_1 which has its midpoint on the axis).
d) Shade the area between the extreme rays (i.e. rays through the top and bottom of the objective lens) from one point. (This indicates the region through which all rays must pass if they come from that point.)
e) Mark the place where all possible rays from the object which pass through the telescope are concentrated into the smallest area (this area is called the **eye ring** or exit pupil). ■

The eye ring is the best position for the eye, since it is the place where most light can be received and where the observer has the widest field of view. In figure 3.16, the objective of a telescope is illuminated by light diffused by a ground glass screen. Rays from point A at the top of the objective lens converge to A_1 after passing through the eyepiece. A_1 is the real image of A; similarly, B_1 is the image of B. The eye ring or exit pupil is the image of the objective formed by the eyepiece.

Q 3.35 Study question

Show, by referring to figure 3.16, that for a telescope in normal adjustment the angular magnification M is given by

$$M = \frac{\text{diameter of objective}}{\text{diameter of eye ring}}$$

Indicate briefly how you would check this result experimentally. ■

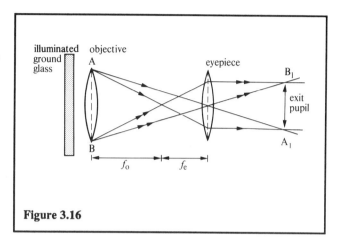

Figure 3.16

Q 3.36 Self-assessment question

(a) Why is it pointless to design a telescope with an exit pupil greater than about 2 mm (the diameter of the pupil of the eye)?
(b) An astronomical telescope is to be constructed from two converging lenses of focal lengths 96 cm and 4.0 cm. What will be the location of the eye ring?
(c) Suggest an appropriate diameter for the objective lens. ■

In designing a telescope, the diameter of the objective must be related to the magnifying power, to produce the right size of eye ring. Large diameter objectives are desirable, because

1 the resolving power (the ability to separate close objects and observe fine detail) increases with the diameter of the objective (see topic 5), and,
2 a large objective collects more light.

Have you ever considered why a street lamp 50 m away looks just as bright as one 25 m away? Less light reaches your eye from the distant lamp, only a quarter as much as from the near lamp, because light spreads out from the source. But the visual angle for the distant lamp is half that for the near lamp. The image of the distant lamp on the retina is half as high and half as wide as that of the near lamp, so a quarter of the light is focused into a quarter of the area on the retina. The 'energy density' (light energy per unit area) is the same for both images, so the eye sees both street lamps as equally bright.

A telescope receives light through an objective lens and transmits it to the observer's eye. Think about the brightness of the images it produces.

Other telescopes

Reflecting telescopes use a concave mirror of long focal length as the objective instead of a lens, though the principle is the same as for refracting telescopes. The largest modern astronomical telescopes are reflectors as they are easier to construct and do not suffer from the aberrations of images which occur with large lenses.

Terrestrial telescopes differ from astronomical ones by arranging for the final image to be the right way up. This can be achieved by means of an 'erecting' lens, or by the use of totally internally reflecting prisms. For practical purposes the use of prisms is more convenient, as they make a small compact instrument. These telescopes are usually mounted in pairs and are known as prismatic binoculars.

An earlier form of terrestrial telescope was made by Galileo in 1609. He used a diverging lens instead of a converging lens as the eyepiece. This instrument does not produce a high magnification. When two are mounted as a pair they are described as 'opera glasses'.

Radio telescopes are important in contemporary astronomy because much of the radiation coming from space is of much longer wavelength than light, in the 'radio wave' part of the electromagnetic spectrum (see topic 4). Many, like the well-known one at Jodrell Bank, Cheshire, have a recognisable reflector or 'dish' which can be steered. Others have a set of aerials distributed over a wide area (figure 3.17).

Figure 3.17

A further study of the use of telescopes in astronomy can be found in the topic option 'Physics of Astronomy' in the *Student's resource book*.

The compound microscope

The magnifying glass is sometimes referred to as a simple microscope. A compound microscope obtains magnification in two stages. The objective is a converging lens of short focal length. If an object is placed just a little more than the focal length from the objective then an enlarged real image is produced. This image becomes the object for a second lens, the eyepiece, which acts as a simple magnifying glass. The final image produced by the eyepiece is located at the near point.

Figure 3.18 shows a ray from the top of an object passing through the optical centre of the objective and refracted at the eyepiece. An image I_1 is produced by the objective at a distance v from the eyepiece, and the image I_2 is produced by the eyepiece. The line through the centre of the eyepiece is a construction line, to enable image I_2 to be drawn to the correct size (a ray from the top of I_1 could travel along this line through the centre of the lens).

In a microscope, the distance between the objective and eyepiece is fixed and the microscope is focused by moving the whole microscope relative to the fixed object.

Q 3.37 Self-assessment question

If the microscope is used for prolonged observation, it is more restful for the eye to view a final image at infinity. How can the microscope shown in figure 3.18 be refocused to produce a final image at infinity? Explain your answer, stating how object and image distances change when the microscope tube is moved. ■

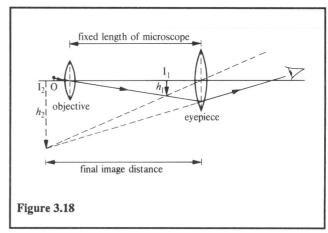

Figure 3.18

The angular magnification M for a microscope, simple or compound, is given by

$$M = \frac{\beta}{\alpha}$$

where β is the visual angle for the final image produced by the microscope, and α is the visual angle when the object is at the near point.

Q 3.38 Development question

Use figure 3.18 and the above definition to show that angular magnification M = linear magnification produce by objective × linear magnification produced by eyepiece × D/v, where D is the least distance of distinct vision and v is the final image distance. ■

As with telescopes, we can explain the principle of the microscope by drawing the paths of rays through the system. These diagrams are not construction diagrams to locate image positions for particular lenses, but show the optical system for any microscope. Appropriate positions are chosen for the object and images and construction lines are used to determine their correct sizes for those locations.

Q 3.39 Study question

(a) Draw a diagram showing the paths through a microscope of three rays from the top of a small object which lies across the axis with its midpoint on the axis. The rays should pass through the centre, top and bottom of the objective.
(b) Draw three rays through the microscope from the bottom of the object.
(c) Locate the images formed, and distinguish clearly between construction lines and actual rays.
(d) Mark the eye ring. ■

Q 3.40 Self-assessment question

A compound microscope has an objective lens of focal length 40 mm, and an eyepiece of focal length 60 mm, separated by 250 mm. An object 2.0 mm long is set up 50 mm from the objective lens.

(a) Calculate the position and size of the image formed by the objective lens.

(b) Calculate the position and size of the final image formed by the eyepiece.

(c) Calculate the angular magnification produced by the microscope. ■

The converging lens

Apparatus

○ converging lens and holder
○ plane mirror
○ cross-wires
○ lamp and holder
○ screen
○ metre rule

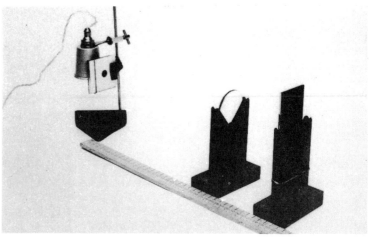

Figure 3.19

Using an auxiliary plane mirror

1 First find an approximate value for the focal length of the lens by focusing the image of a distant object (e.g a laboratory window) on the screen. Measure the distance between the lens and the screen. This is a rough value of the focal length of the lens.

2 Place the illuminated cross-wires at a distance from the lens equal to the approximate focal length and position the plane mirror behind the lens, normal to the principal axis (figure 3.19).

3 Adjust the position of the cross-wires until a sharp image of the cross-wires is formed alongside them.

4 Measure the distance of the cross-wires from the optical centre of the lens. This is the focal length f of the lens.

5 Repeat steps 3 and 4 several times and find the mean of the results.

6 Explain, with the aid of a ray diagram, why the distance from the object to the lens is equal to the focal length of the lens when the object and image coincide.

7 Does the position of the plane mirror make any difference to your result? Give a reason.

Graphical method

1 Place the illuminated cross-wires at a distance from the lens of approximately $2f$. Adjust the position of the screen so that there is a sharp image on the screen.

2 Measure the distances of the object, u, and the image, v, from the lens.

3 Move the object 2 cm nearer the lens and locate the new position of the image. Obtain at least five sets of readings of the object distance and the image distance. Note: Because of the reversibility of light all corresponding values of u and v may be interchanged thus, in effect, doubling your readings.

4 Plot graphs of (i) v (y-axis) against u (x-axis), and (ii) $1/v$ (y-axis) against $1/u$ (x-axis). Comment on these graphs and explain what you think they show.

Note. You may have to take additional readings to obtain appropriately spaced points on these graphs.

The equation

$$\frac{1}{v} = -\ \frac{1}{u} + \frac{1}{f}$$

indicates a gradient of 1 and equal intercepts on the axes.

5 What is the value of v when $u = v$? How is this value related to the focal length of the lens? How can you obtain the focal length of the lens from the graph of v against u? Write down the answer that you obtain.

6 What is the value of $1/v$ when $1/u$ is zero? How can you obtain the focal length of the lens from the graph of $1/v$ against $1/u$? (You should obtain the mean of two values.)

EXPERIMENT WV 9
The astronomical telescope

Apparatus

○ long focal length converging lens (50 cm)
○ short focal length converging lens (10 cm)
○ suitable mounting rod
○ metre rule
○ low voltage lamp and power supply
○ tissue paper or greaseproof paper
○ screen

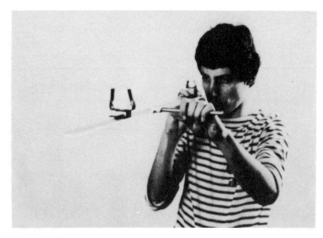

Figure 3.20

Constructing the telescope

1 Determine the focal lengths of each lens by focusing the image of a distant object on a screen.

2 Place a lamp at the far side of the laboratory. Mount the lens with the longer focal length at one end of the mounting rod. Point the rod at the lamp and locate the image of the lamp on a piece of greaseproof paper.

3 Attach the second lens near the other end of the mounting rod. Adjust the position of this lens so that it acts as a magnifying glass for the image on the greaseproof paper.

4 Remove the greaseproof paper and look directly at the image of the lamp formed by the telescope (figure 3.20).

Estimating the magnification

1 Rule several horizontal lines, 2 cm apart, on a sheet of paper or a blackboard. Illuminate the lines with a lamp.

2 Point the telescope towards the ruled lines (which should be on the far side of the laboratory) and adjust the position of the eyepiece until the lines can be seen clearly.

3 Look through the telescope with one eye and look directly at the lines with the other (unaided) eye. Make final adjustments to the eyepiece until the eye looking through the telecope sees the image clearly in focus, while the unaided eye sees the lines clearly in focus. You must make a conscious effort to relax your eyes. Don't give up immediately!

4 Count how many lines, as viewed directly, lie between two adjacent lines as seen through the telescope. Hence estimate the magnification produced by your telescope.

5 Compare your results with the value obtained from the formula

$$\text{angular magnification} = \frac{\text{focal length of object}}{\text{focal length of eyepiece}}$$

Which gives the value for the angular mangification if both the object and image are an infinite distance from the eye (normal adjustment).

Locating the eye ring

1 Place a piece of greaseproof paper (or a frosted glass screen) close to the objective. Illuminate it with light from a lamp, and position a piece of white card behind the eyepiece. You should observe a circle of light.

2 Adjust the position of the card until the circle has a sharp outline. Of what is the circle the image?

3 Measure the diameter d of this image and the diameter D of the objective lens. Find the ratio D/d. This ratio is numerically equal to the angular magnification of the telescope, when it is in normal adjustment.

Questions on objectives

1 Figure 3.21 shows an optical dipstick. It consists of a perspex probe with a prismatic tip, with a lamp and a photocell mounted at the top. When the probe is in air, light from the lamp passes down the probe, is *totally internally reflected* twice at the prismatic end, returns up the probe and is reflected to the photocell. When the tip of the probe is immersed in a liquid, the *critical angle* is altered. Total internal reflection does not take place, and the beam no longer returns up the probe. The photocell, therefore, receives less light, its electrical resistance increases, and a signal is passed to the control box.

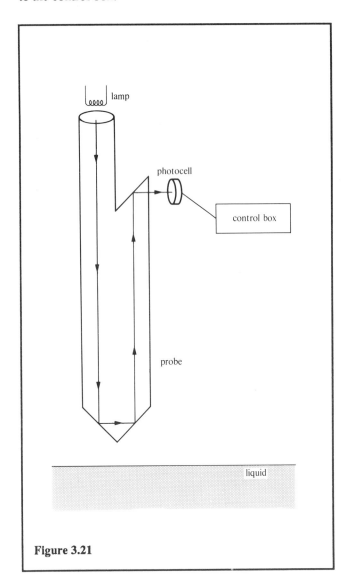

Figure 3.21

(a) Explain what is meant by total internal reflection and critical angle.
(b) Why does the critical angle change when the probe is immersed in a liquid (e.g. water) whose refractive index is less than that of perspex? Why does the beam no longer pass up the probe?
(c) Calculate the critical angle for the passage of light from perspex to air (the refractive index of perspex is 1.5).
(d) What happens to the light when the probe is immersed in a liquid whose refractive index is greater than that of perspex?

(objectives 1, 3 and 10)

2 A beaker contains water to a depth of 80 mm, and above that a 40 mm layer of oil.
(a) Draw a ray diagram to show how an eye looking vertically down into the beaker sees the image of a point on the bottom of the beaker.
(b) Calculate the distance of this image below the upper surface of the oil. (The refractive indices of water and oil relative to air are respectively 1.33 and 1.45.)

(objectives 5 and 10)

3 A thin converging lens produces a sharp image of the object on a screen. If the distance between the object and image is d and the magnification obtained is m, find an expression for the focal length of the lens.

(objectives 6 and 10)

4 Draw labelled ray diagrams to illustrate the methods used to measure the focal length of (i) a thin converging lens with the aid of a plane mirror, and (ii) a thin diverging lens with the aid of a thin converting lens of longer focal length. In each case, show how to calculate the result.

(objective 7)

5 Explain what is meant by the angular magnification M of an astronomical telescope.

(objective 2)

6 Which of the following expressions is the correct relationship for the angular magnification of an astronomical telescope in normal adjustment, where f_o and f_e are the focal lengths of the objective and eyepiece respectively?

A f_o/f_e **B** f_e/f_o **C** $f_o \times f_e$ **D** $f_o + f_e$ **E** $f_o - f_e$

(objective 8)

7 (a) Define angular magnification, as applied to a microscope.
(b) Draw a diagram to show the passage of three rays of light through a compound microscope from a non-axial point, the final image being formed at the least distance of distinct vision. Mark clearly the principal foci of the objective and eyepiece lenses.

(objective 9)

TOPIC 4

Electromagnetic waves

Study time 0.5 - 1 week

Summary

We shall use the field-line model to explain the nature of electromagnetic radiation. The polarisation of light supports the model and has useful applications in chemistry, geology and engineering. Stress concentration can be seen in this perspex model of a railway bridge.

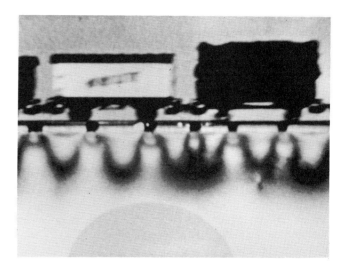

Objectives

When you have completed this topic you should be able to:

1 Use the following scientific terms correctly: electromagnetic waves, the electromagnetic spectrum, source and detection (of e.m. waves), scattering, plane of vibration, plane-polarised light, partially polarised light, unpolarised light, polariser, crossed arrangement, analyser, Polaroid, double refraction, selective absorption, photoelasticity, optical activity.

2 Outline briefly the nature of electromagnetic waves.

3 Describe the main types of radiations in the electromagnetic spectrum including their approximate range of wavelengths.

4 Outline the methods of production and detection and the properties of different radiations in the electromagnetic spectrum.

5 Describe a terrestrial method of measuring the speed of light.

6 Outline the methods for producing plane-polarised light by reflection and by selective absorption.

7 Describe the applications of the use of plane-polarised light, including the polarimeter and the strain gauge.

Experiments

WV 10 Polarisation of microwaves (optional)   (0.5 hour)
WV 11 Polarisation of light waves   (0.75 hour)
WV 12 Investigating stress (optional)   (0.75 hour)

References

Akrill   Chapter 28
Bolton   Chapter 10
Duncan   Chapter 20
Muncaster   Chapters 27 and 28
Nelkon   Chapters 21
Whelan   Chapters 37 and 40

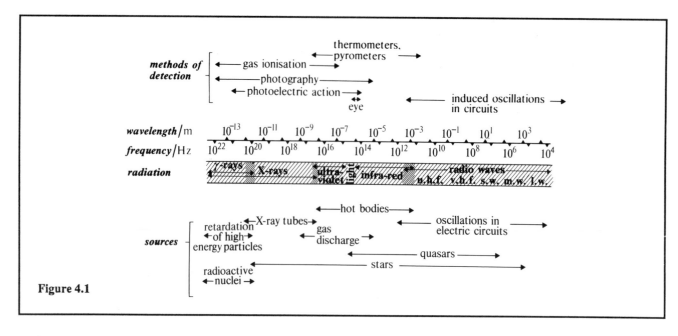

Figure 4.1

4.1 The electromagnetic spectrum

The light waves you have been studying in the last topic are one of the forms of radiation which we call electromagnetic waves. When we observe the spectrum of light from the sun we are dealing with only a very small part of its energy radiation spectrum. Most of the energy reaching the earth from the sun is invisible, but we are made aware of this invisible radiation by its effects. Our environment of animal and plant life depends on the continual radiation of the sun's wide spectrum, visible and invisible, of electromagnetic waves.

Figure 4.1 shows the full spectrum of electromagnetic waves, the sources of different kinds of radiation and the various detectors used. This figure summarises a great deal of information, much of which is covered in this topic. We will refer back to it in later sections.

Speed of electromagnetic radiation

One piece of information not included in figure 4.1 is the speed of electromagnetic radiation c. The first value of the speed of light was obtained by Roemer, in 1675, and measurements of increasing accuracy have continued to be made ever since. (See *Student's resource book*, section 2, on experimental errors.)

Measurement of the speed of light in different media was needed to test Huygens' and Newton's explanations of refraction. This was obtained, in 1860, by Foucault.

As the nature of light became better understood, the importance of its speed in a vacuum became more obvious. It was realised that this speed c was one of the most important constants in the universe. It was the speed, not just of light, but of all electromagnetic waves in a vacuum. The speed of light squared c^2 was found to relate mass and energy in the special theory of relativity. This is covered in the unit *Electrons and the nucleus*.

The internationally accepted value of c is

$$299\ 792\ 459.0 \pm 0.8\ \text{m s}^{-1}$$

Because light travels at such a high speed, the time intervals to be measured are very small, even when the light is timed over large distances. Early methods measured its speed over astronomical distances. As timing methods were improved, the distance of travel was reduced to the order of a metre.

Two main terrestrial methods have been used:

1 'Chopped' light beam methods: measuring the transit time for short light pulses between leaving and returning through a gate, such as the gap in a toothed wheel (Fizeau's method, 1899) or an electric shutter (Anderson's method using a Kerr cell, 1941).

2 Rotating mirror methods: measuring transit time by reflecting light from a rotating mirror at the beginning and end of its measured path.

Q 4.1 Study question

Describe, with a diagram, one terrestrial method of measuring the speed of light, explaining which quantities are measured, and how a relationship is derived for the velocity of light. Give a set of typical values for the various quantities which appear in the relationship. ■

Electromagnetic waves share many general wave properties with other types of waves, but they also form a family of waves with properties which are particular to electromagnetic waves.

Q 4.2 Self-assessment question

(a) State three properties of electromagnetic waves which are shared with mechanical waves.
(b) State three particular properties of electromagnetic waves. (Figure 4.1 provides some clues, but make sure your answer applies to *all* electromagnetic waves.)
(c) State the one factor which distinguishes one kind of electromagnetic wave from another. ■

You have already examined convincing evidence that light is a wave, but it is difficult to visualise such a wave. Can we talk of crests and troughs for a light wave? What is it, if anything, that is 'going up and down' in the wave? A clue is found by remembering that light waves are emitted when electrons move between energy levels and the absorption of light energy can produce a movement of electrons to new energy levels.

Q 4.3 Development question

What can exert a force on an electron? ∎

The most obvious answers to this question are electric and magnetic fields. So, a possible wave model for light is that it is an 'electric field wave'. Equally possible is 'a magnetic field wave'. Fortunately, we don't have to choose between these: it turns out to be both.

4.2 The nature of electromagnetic waves

Let us discover why the name *electromagnetic* is appropriate for the family of waves which includes light waves.

Consider first what happens in a changing magnetic field. If a magnet is moved near a coil, we can detect an induced current in the coil. A current cannot flow unless there is an electric field set up to move charge around the wire and the conventional current direction (the direction in which positive charge may flow) indicates the direction of the electric field. This field is produced by the moving magnet even if the coil is not there (figure 4.2). *Therefore, a changing magnetic field produces a changing electric field at right angles to the direction in which the magnetic field changes.*

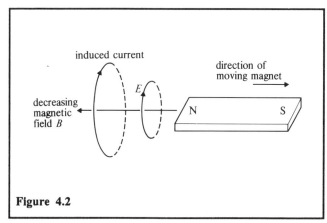

Figure 4.2

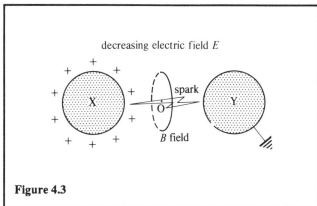

Figure 4.3

Now consider the changing electric field produced when a positively charged sphere X (figure 4.3) is discharged to an earthed sphere Y by a spark.

Q 4.4 Development question*

(a) What is the direction of the electric field at point O, between X and Y? Is it an increasing or a decreasing field?
(b) As the charge flows between X and Y, the electric field decreases and also a magnetic field *B* is produced around the charge flow. Describe the direction of the *B*-field (i) as viewed from X, (ii) in relation to the *E*-field. ∎

We can say that *a changing electric field produces a magnetic field which is perpendicular to the direction in which the electric field changes.*

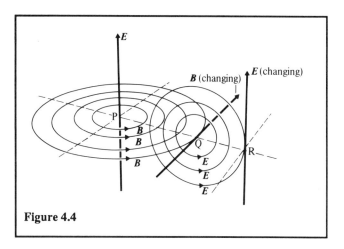

Figure 4.4

Now suppose there is a *variable vertical electric field* at point P (see figure 4.4). This will produce a *horizontal magnetic field* around P. At a point Q some distance from P there is a *varying magnetic field*.

Q 4.5 Development question*

(a) Is the *B*-field at Q horizontal or vertical?
(b) The varying *B*-field at Q produces a varying electric field around Q. In what plane is the electric field around Q?
(c) What is the direction of the changing electric field at R? ∎

So we see that a changing vertical electric field at P will result in a changing vertical field at R. There is, however, a time lag between the change in the field at P and the resulting effect at R. If the electric field at one point varies periodically, then the electric field at a distant point will also vary periodically, but a little later in time. The result is the propagation of a wave, and we have a good analogy in the setting up of waves on the surface of water by a vibrating dipper. After a time lapse, the water surface some distance away from the dipper vibrates as a wave is propagated. Of course, the varying magnetic field at P will also produce, after a time lapse, a varying magnetic field at R.

Changing electric and magnetic fields travel together from the source and an electromagnetic wave is propagated. Figure 4.5 represents an e.m. wave in which *E*- and *B*-fields vary sinusoidally.

Note. An electromagnetic wave is the movement through space of a varying electric field accompanied by a varying magnetic field and each changing field is perpendicular to the direction of propagation of the wave. Electromagnetic waves are thus *transverse* waves.

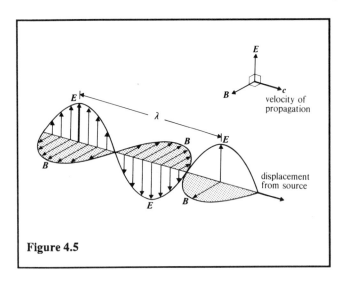

Figure 4.5

The principles discussed above of the interdependence of electric and magnetic fields were the assumptions on which James Clerk Maxwell based his mathematical theory (published in 1873) that electrical disturbances with associated magnetic changes are propagated in space with a speed of $1/\varepsilon_0\mu_0$, where ε_0 and μ_0 are the permittivity and permeability of free space respectively (see the unit *Forces and fields*).

The surprising fact emerged that this velocity was very close to the speed of light measured by Fizeau in 1849. The conclusion Maxwell came to was that light itself was an electromagnetic disturbance in the form of waves and that other similar radiations must exist. One of these 'other radiations' was discovered in 1888, when Heinrich Hertz produced radio waves using a spark transmitter. This development of knowledge about electromagnetic waves emphasises the important complementary roles of theoretical and experimental scientists.

EXTENSION

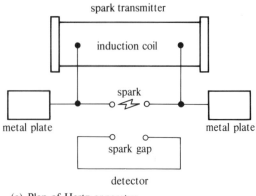

(a) Plan of Hertz apparatus

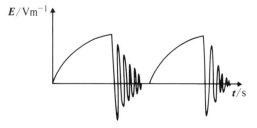

(b) Oscillating electric field in spark gap of transmitter

Hertz's spark transmitter (figure 4.6a) is essentially a capacitor which is charged up by an induction coil. Charging of the capacitor continues until the p.d. across the spark gap produces a breakdown potential gradient ($300\,\mathrm{V\,mm^{-1}}$) and a spark is produced. The spark oscillates very rapidly in the narrow ionised air gap (see figure 4.6b) producing an oscillating electric field E until the ions are collected and charging up starts again.

Hertz wrote: '*I tried whether the observed electrical disturbances did not manifest effects of corresponding magnitude in neighbouring conductors. I therefore bent some copper wire into the form of rectangular circuits, about 10-20 cm in the side, and containing only very short spark-gaps ... when the rectangle was brought sufficiently near, a stream of sparks in it always accompanied the discharges of the induction coil...*'

Q 4.6 Self-assessment question

Describe in your own words how this observation showed the presence of electromagnetic waves. ∎

Figure 4.6

4.3 Properties of electromagnetic waves

All the recorded properties of different electromagnetic waves can be explained using the same basic physics, provided we make adjustments for differences in frequency. Frequency has two effects:

1 The size of the packets of energy in which the radiation is emitted depends on frequency, and the higher frequency radiations are emitted in larger energy packets (**photons**).

This is discussed fully in the unit *Electrons and the nucleus*. It provides an explanation of why X-rays are more penetrating than light in metals and can ionise gases, and why a faint beam of light can affect a photographic plate whilst the powerful energy emission of a radio station produces no effect on a film.

2 Frequency (with speed) also determines wavelength, and the properties of waves depend on the comparative sizes of the wavelength and interacting matter. This means that a

mountain is the same kind of obstacle to a long radio wave as a pinhead is to a wave of light.

It is important to note that there are no very precise boundaries between different types of waves, and some ranges overlap. Properties will obviously vary within a particular named range (e.g. between long and short infra-red), but there will be no abrupt change in properties between two different types of wave which have similar frequencies.

Waves of wavelength 10^{-10} m have exactly the same properties whether we call them X-rays (because they are produced by slowing down electrons) or gamma rays (because they come from an excited nucleus).

Fences around missile warning radar stations prevent cattle being cooked prematurely, though they may end up eventually as steak cooked in a microwave oven! This reminds us of the fact that infra-red waves and microwaves used in radar both share similar heating properties.

Q 4.7 Self-assessment question

X-rays can ionise gases, light waves cannot. Explain this, and suggest (with a reason) which of the two types of radiation will be more penetrating in air. ■

Sources and detectors

The **source** of wave energy emission moves from outside the atom to the nucleus as we move through the spectrum from long to short waves.

Radio waves are produced by oscillations of free electrons in matter; infra-red waves result from changes in the vibrational energy of molecules; visible and ultraviolet radiation are produced by energy changes in outer electrons in the atom; X-rays are produced by energy changes of inner orbital electrons and by the slowing down of fast electrons; γ-rays are produced by energy changes within the nucleus.

Detectors use any suitable property of the wave. Notice (figure 4.1) that ionisation, photography and heating effects are all used for a wide range of radiation. Light waves probably have the largest selection of detectors and, of course, include one - the eye - which is unique.

Q 4.8 Study question

Study figure 4.1 and any references in your books to the electromagnetic spectrum.
(a) Make a list of the different types of radiation in this spectrum in order of wavelength and for each type name one source and one kind of detector.
(b) List any properties which are used for detecting more than one kind of radiation, saying which kinds are detected in this common way. ■

The origin of γ-rays and the production of X-rays are studied in detail in the unit *Electrons and the nucleus*.

Reflection, refraction, transmission

Media transparent to one wave are opaque to others. Glass is not transparent for most ultraviolet and infra-red radiation, but quartz can transmit ultraviolet and rock salt can transmit

infra-red. Special filters are used in photography to prevent ultraviolet rays reaching the film because the glass of the lens is transparent to some ultraviolet with wavelengths near to the visible region.

Q 4.9 Self-assessment question

Which property of waves is used for the location and guidance of ships and aircraft? What kind of waves are used? ■

Read the following description of an application for electromagnetic waves, then answer question 4.10.

Partially deaf children are able to benefit from a new development in hearing aids designed for use in schools. Audio frequency signals are carried by electromagnetic waves of frequencies between 200 and 280 GHz and the hearing aid worn by a child consists of a small receiver carried on the chest, and headphones. The electromagnetic waves are radiated into the classroom from a transmitter in the teacher's desk and also from four transmitters mounted in each corner of the room. The child's receiver is designed to give good reception in any position in the room. Stereo audio signals are used so that the separate channels can be set at the receiver to cater for each child's particular disability. The advantage of using these particular carrier waves is that interference between adjacent classrooms is impossible. In more conventional systems for the hard-of-hearing in schools, such interference can be a severe problem.

Q 4.10 Self-assessment question

(a) What name is given to this frequency range of electromagnetic radiation? (See figure 4.1.)
(b) What property of these waves, not possessed by radio waves, makes interference impossible between classrooms? ■

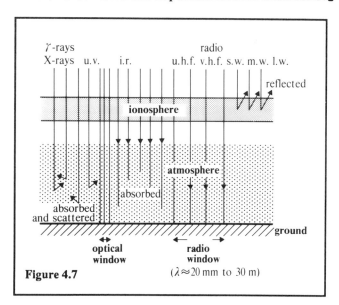

Figure 4.7

Figure 4.7 shows how radiation from space is affected by the earth's atmosphere and the ion layer above it. It shows that there are only two windows (frequency ranges) open to receive light and very short radio waves. The upper atmosphere (ionosphere) is opaque to other radio frequencies.

In fact, long distance radio reception depends upon the reflection of radio waves from a layer of charged particles high in the ionosphere.

Q 4.11 Self-assessment question

Suggest suitable wavelengths for radio communication between London and Australia using
(a) a communications satellite system,
(b) ionospheric reflection. ■

Q 4.12 Self-assessment question

A radio receiver 150 km from a short-wave transmitter (broadcasting 30 m waves) receives two waves which are superposed at the receiver. One wave is diffracted around the earth's surface (the ground wave) and one is reflected from the ionosphere (the sky wave). Explain how continual changes in the ionospheric layer can produce fading (varying strength) reception at the receiver. Explain why the reception could be better at much greater distances from the transmitter. ■

Scattering

Light waves are scattered by gas molecules and tiny particles (smoke or dust). When a light wave impinges on an atom or molecule, the vibrating *E*-field interacts with the electrons producing a forced oscillation of the whole molecule which, therefore, absorbs some of the wave energy. The vibrating molecule will re-radiate energy in all directions, and this effect is known as **scattering**. The natural frequency of a typical vibrating molecule is in the ultraviolet region. If the incident light frequency is near to that of ultraviolet, the forced vibrations will be close to resonance and so a lot of energy will be absorbed and re-radiated (scattered). Longer wavelengths of light will produce less scattering; in fact, the degree of scattering is proportional to the fourth power of the frequency.

Particles of larger size (e.g. smoke particles) also produce scattering which is partly a diffraction effect and partly a reflection of waves. If the particles are smaller than the wavelength of light, long visible waves will be affected very little but the short waves will behave as though the particles were big obstacles and, as a result, short waves will be scattered more than long waves. If the particles are bigger than the wavelength of red light, then all visible waves treat the particles as big obstacles and all wavelengths are scattered significantly. The degree of scattering is independent of wavelength.

Q 4.13 Self-assessment question

(a) Give a reason why tobacco smoke appears blue but the 'steam' from a kettle is white.
(b) Why is the sky blue? What does an astronaut observe about the colour of the sun and sky as he moves up through the atmosphere?
(c) A camera using a film which is sensitive to infra-red rays can take a picture through a mist. Explain briefly why this is so. ■

Interference and diffraction

The work on the ripple tank in section 1.4 showed how two or more waves can interact to change their total intensity at a point. The intensity variation depends on the amplitude. If the two waves are in phase (both 'crests' or 'troughs', for example) the resultant amplitude is the sum of the two; if they

are out of phase, it is the difference between them (which will result in zero amplitude if the two waves are the same.

You will also have seen that the diffraction of a wave (its bending at one edge or through an aperture) also depends on the wavelength. Bending is only observed to a substantial extent if the aperture is about the same size as the wavelength, or smaller.

This means that we are much more aware of diffraction and interference effects of long waves than short waves.

Radio waves have the longest wavelength and so within the e.m. spectrum interference and diffraction effects are most noticeable.

Q 4.14 Self-assessment question

People living near to an airport flight-path may get 'pulsing' of the television signal. With the help of figure 4.8 explain the cause of this 'pulsing' and describe what will be observed on the television screen. ■

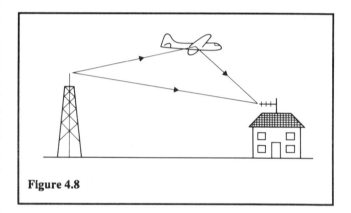

Figure 4.8

Q 4.15 Self-assessment question

Many telephone calls are now carried by radio waves. Very short wavelength waves (microwaves) have to be used because these waves can carry many more simultaneous messages than long radio waves. There are, however, problems to be overcome in transmitting microwaves. What are these particular problems and how are they overcome to provide a nationwide radio-telephone system? ■

C Comprehension WV 2
Wavy radio

This is a report of interference on BBC Radio 2.

At the other end of the spectrum X-rays have a wavelength which is of the same order of magnitude as the distance between atoms in a crystal.

In 1912 Von Laue first suggested that a crystal should act as a three-dimensional diffraction grating. Figure 4.9 shows the diffraction pattern (Laue pattern) produced on a photographic plate by sending non-monochromatic X-rays through a crystal using the method shown in the figure. This experiment by Laue and his colleagues provided convincing evidence that X-rays are waves.

The particular Laue pattern produced using a crystal as a transmission diffraction grating is determined by the crystal structure, but its analysis proved very difficult.

Sir William Bragg and his son Sir Lawrence Bragg developed a simpler technique for crystal analysis. This has become a standard technique for determining crystal structure, and is described in the unit *Behaviour of materials*. There is a comprehension exercise on the work of the Braggs in the *Student's resource book*.

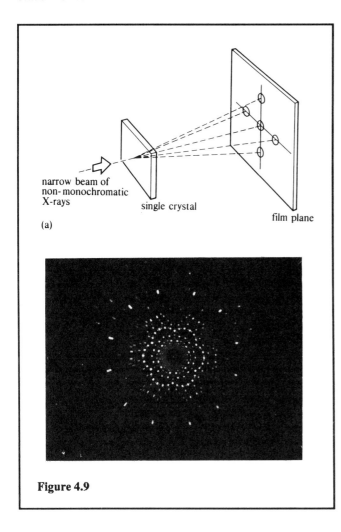

narrow beam of non-monochromatic X-rays

single crystal

film plane

(a)

Figure 4.9

The diffraction and interference of light are also important phenomena, which need certain conditions to be fulfilled to be observed. We will study these in the next topic.

Q 4.16 Study question

For each of the seven named ranges of e.m. waves: γ-rays, X-rays, ultraviolet, visible, infra-red, microwave and radio, give
(a) any characteristic properties which distinguish one range from another,
(b) applications in each particular range. ■

4.4 Polarisation

In the previous section it was shown that e.m. waves are transverse. The electric and magnetic fields vary in directions which are perpendicular to the direction of propagation of the wave (figure 4.5).

Unpolarised and plane-polarised waves

Figure 4.5 represents an electromagnetic wave in which the plane containing the electric vector is fixed. It is, therefore, described as a **plane-polarised wave**. Such a wave can be represented by simple diagrams (figure 4.10), which each indicate the plane containing the electric vector and the direction of propagation (called the **plane of vibration**).

The arrows show the direction of the varying electrical field vector E. The magnetic field direction is not indicated, since we can always assume its presence and direction and it is the electric field which is more involved in the interaction between electromagnetic waves and atoms.

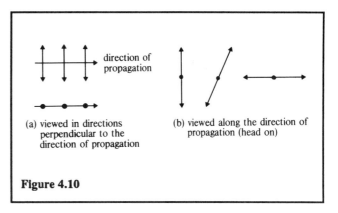

direction of propagation

(a) viewed in directions perpendicular to the direction of propagation

(b) viewed along the direction of propagation (head on)

Figure 4.10

Many electromagnetic waves are propagated as a group of numerous individual wave pulses travelling together. For example, light is emitted as the result of the acceleration of electrons in many atoms of the source and these accelerations occur at random producing a light beam made up of many pulses, each pulse having a different plane of vibration for its electric vector field. We can represent this kind of radiation diagrammatically as shown in figure 4.11. An electromagnetic wave whose electric field vectors vary randomly with time in both magnitude and direction is an **unpolarised** wave.

Each of the electric vectors shown in figure 4.11 can be resolved into two component vibrations in planes at right angles to each other. By adding together all these components of random vibrations and averaging with time, an unpolarised wave can be considered as equivalent to a pair of superposed plane-polarised waves with the same average amplitude (but with a random phase difference). Thus, figure 4.12 shows ways of representing an unpolarised wave showing the two *major equal components* of E at right angles.

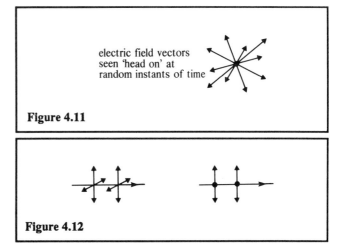

electric field vectors seen 'head on' at random instants of time

Figure 4.11

Figure 4.12

If one of these major component electric vibrations can be removed, an unpolarised wave can be converted into a plane-polarised wave with all the electric field vibrations in one plane, the plane of vibration.

If one of the major components of an unpolarised wave is not removed completely but reduced in magnitude, the wave is described as a **partially polarised** wave.

E Experiment WV 10 (optional)
Polarisation of microwaves

In this experiment you will investigate how the polarisation of 3 cm radio waves can be analysed.

Polarisation of light waves

The human eye cannot distinguish between plane-polarised and unpolarised light. There is evidence that some other living things (e.g. bees) can detect the polarisation of light - a fact which provides an explanation of the guidance system of bees. If we are to detect and analyse the polarisation of light waves, we need the help of analysers like Polaroid.

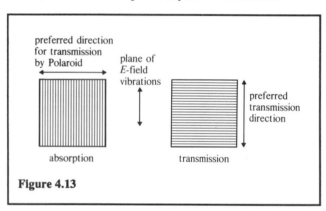

Figure 4.13

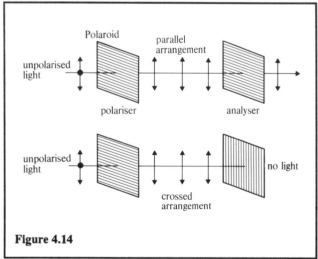

Figure 4.14

Polaroid is made up of long chain molecules to which iodine atoms are attached. The presence of iodine allows electrons to move along the chains. The chains are aligned in one direction so that they behave like a fine grille of conducting wires which prevent transmission of any light with the electric field E vibrating parallel to the long chains (figure 4.13). (In experiment WV 10 you observed how a grille of

metal wires could absorb microwaves whose plane of vibration was parallel to the wires.) If the electric field vibrates across the chains, light is transmitted.

Figure 4.14 shows a sheet of Polaroid used as a **polariser** (converting unpolarised light into plane-polarised light). The figure also shows how a second Polaroid can be used as an **analyser** to locate the plane of polarisation. As the analysing Polaroid is rotated, the transmitted light changes from maximum to zero (this is true for 'ideal' Polaroid but, in practice, there is no complete extinction although high quality Polaroid comes close to the ideal). When the Polaroids are **crossed**, their preferred directions for transmission are at right angles.

E Experiment WV 11
Polarisation of light waves

The aim is to produce plane polarised light and analyse it with polaroid.

Q 4.17 Study question*

A piece of Polaroid which is being used as an analyser is rotated through an angle θ from the parallel position (shown in figure 4.14). Sketch the face of the Polaroid marking in the angle θ and the direction of the E-field vibrations. Hence show that the transmitted light intensity is proportional to $\cos^2 \theta$. ∎

Q 4.18 Self-assessment question

The dazzling effect of the headlights of approaching traffic is a hazard for night drivers. It has been suggested that the use of Polaroid filters for headlights and driving glasses could overcome the hazard. Can you suggest how the Polaroid can be arranged so that a driver sees his own headlight beam but is not dazzled by other cars? ∎

When light falls on certain crystals (e.g. calcite, quartz) two refracted beams are produced travelling at different speeds in the crystal. It is found that the two beams are each plane-polarised with electric fields vibrating at right angles. This is called **double refraction**. Some of these doubly refracting crystals absorb the energy of one of these beams and so transmit plane-polarised light. The crystals used in making Polaroid have a similar ability of selectively absorbing one component of light.

Some transparent materials exhibit double refraction when subjected to stress and their use in stress analysis is discussed later in this section.

Q 4.19 Study question

You can observe double refraction by placing a large calcite crystal on a page of a book. How could you test whether the two beams are each plane-polarised? Obtain the necessary apparatus and check your suggestion. ∎

Polarisation by reflection

When unpolarised light is reflected from dielectrics (insulators) like glass and water, the reflected light is always partially polarised. Light with the electric vector parallel to the reflecting surface is reflected most strongly.

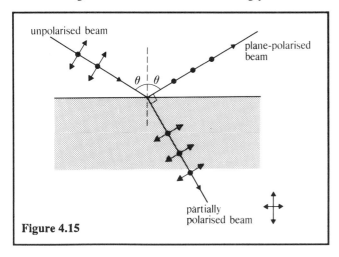

Figure 4.15

If reflected and refracted beams make an angle of 90° with each other, the reflected wave will be plane-polarised (see figure 4.15). This condition occurs at a particular angle of incidence for two given media and a particular wavelength, and this angle is called the polarising angle.

Q 4.20 Self-assessment question

(a) How can Polaroid glasses help to reduce the glare due to reflection of light from the ground?
(b) Why can you see fish in a river better with Polaroid glasses than without? ■

Polarising by scattering

Light waves can only consist of transverse oscillations, and so when an unpolarised wave meets a scattering centre (see figure 4.16) the light scattered through 90° can only have a vibrating E-field in the direction of *one* of the major component E-vectors of the original unpolarised beam; vibrations in the direction of the other component of the unpolarised beam would constitute a longitudinal light wave, which is an impossibility. Thus, light scattered through 90° is plane-polarised.

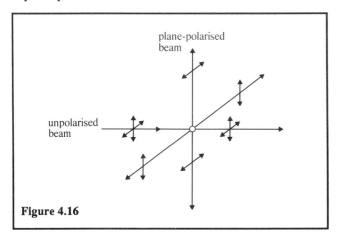

Figure 4.16

Q 4.21 Self-assessment question

Describe how you would obtain evidence from analysis of the light scattered in the atmosphere to support the view that light is a transverse wave. Try out your suggestion. ■

Q 4.22 Self-assessment question

Is the light from a half moon plane-polarised? Give a reason for your answer. ■

Uses of polarised light

The analysis of polarised light provides a versatile tool for chemists, geologists and engineers in studying optically active solutions, minerals and materials under stress.

The experiments in this section provide an opportunity to study two important applications of polarised light, and an explanation of the relevant properties is provided in the text.

Photoelasticity

Glass, perspex, polythene and some other plastics become doubly refracting when subjected to stress. In the unstressed material (e.g. perspex) light of a particular wavelength travels at a fixed speed. In stressed perspex, a plane-polarised incident beam will produce two refracted beams plane-polarised in different planes, one travelling at the unstressed speed and the other travelling more slowly.

The wavelength of the light and the degree of stress determine the speed difference and the resulting phase difference between the two beams. Superposition effects seen when the specimen is viewed through crossed Polaroids depend on the phase difference produced and show dark fringes through lines of equal stress. In white light, coloured fringes are seen. The concentration of fringes can be used to measure the stress. Photoelasticity is used to analyse stress patterns in plastic models of various structures, when loaded, to inform engineers about the areas of stress concentration in the actual large-scale structures.

E Experiment WV 12
Investigating stress (optional)

You will use polarised light to investigate stress in transparent materials.

Certain crystals (e.g. quartz) and liquids (e.g. sugar solution) rotate the plane of vibration of a plane-polarised light wave which passes through them. These substances are called **optically active**. The amount of rotation depends on the concentration of an optically active solution and the length of the light path in the liquid.

Quartz and sodium chlorate crystals, even if only a few mm thick, will rotate the plane of polarisation many degrees. However, sodium chlorate in solution is not optically active, suggesting that the rotating or twisting property in this case depends on the structure of the crystal form. Many organic liquids (e.g. sugar solution) show optical activity which suggests that, in this case, the molecular structure itself is responsible for providing this rotating property.

Q 4.23 Study question

If a chemical reaction involves a change in concentration of an optically active substance the reaction may be followed using the rotation of the plane of polarisation of a light beam.

One such reaction is the inversion of one component of dissolved cane sugar (laevulose) into the oppositely rotating component (dextrose). Hydrogen ions promote the inversion. Set up the arrangement shown in figure 4.17a.

Try an aqueous solution of, say, 30 g per 100 cm³. Devise a means of measuring the angle of rotation of the crossed Polaroid (e.g. figure 4.17b).

Adjust the analyser until the light (from a sodium lamp or flame) is extinguished. Add, say, 5 cm³ of dilute sulphuric acid and start the timing. Record the rotation every minute until it is negligible.

Plot a graph of rotation against time. What is the effect of altering (i) the concentration of sugar, (ii) the quantity of acid, (iii) the temperature? ∎

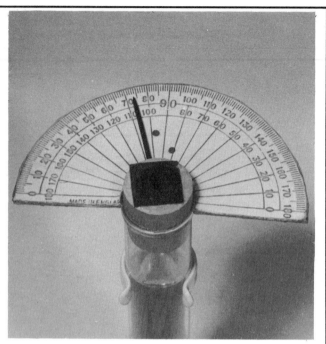

(b)

Figure 4.17   (a)

Polarisation of microwaves (optional)

Apparatus

○ 3 cm wave transmitter
○ 3 cm wave receiver
○ metal grille
○ audio amplifier and loudspeaker (optional)

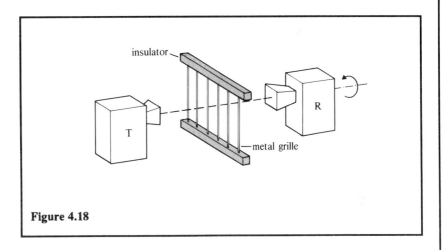

Figure 4.18

The transmitter transmits radio waves of wavelength about 3 cm and these radio waves can be detected by a diode and a meter. Radio waves can be used to carry an audio frequency signal, as happens when radio waves are used to broadcast speech and music. These 3 cm waves can carry an audio frequency signal and an amplifier and speaker attached to the receiver will emit a sound which will indicate the amplitude of the radio waves being received.

The grille has metal rods, about 1.5 cm apart, joined by insulating ends. The grille acts as a selective absorber of radio waves. If the rods are vertical and are placed in a vertical electric field, charges will flow along the rods producing forced oscillations of electrons in the rods, and the wave energy is absorbed. The grille acts as an absorber of all waves with electric vibrations parallel to the grille wires.

1 Set up the transmitter T and receiver R as shown in figure 4.18, without the grille. Observe what happens when R is rotated through 90° in the direction shown. Does the result suggest that the wave from the transmitter is plane-polarised or unpolarised?

2 Insert the grille and observe the effect of rotating it about an axis joining R and T,
(a) when R and T are placed as shown,
(b) when T and R are 'crossed', i.e. with T lying on its side.

3 Use your results to find out
(a) the plane of vibration of the electric waves from the transmitter,
(b) the plane of the electric vibration of waves which the receiver detects.

4 How it is possible with the help of the grille to receive waves in a receiver which is 'crossed' with the transmitter?

5 The grille is *not* a diffraction grating. Can you suggest any reason why this statement seems obviously true?

EXPERIMENT WV 11

Polarisation of light waves

Apparatus

○ lamp
○ 2 Polaroid sheets (or 2 pairs of Polaroid sunglasses)
○ small sheets of glass, metal and polythene
○ transparent tank
○ slide projector

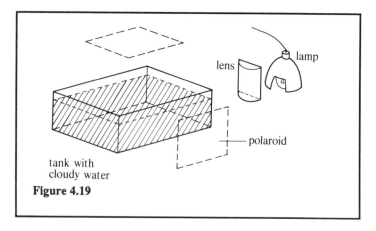

tank with cloudy water

Figure 4.19

1 Look at a light source through a piece of Polaroid (figure 4.19). Rotate the Polaroid about an axis parallel to the beam. Does this affect the intensity of the light transmitted?

2 Fix one piece of Polaroid over the light source and observe the effect of rotating the second Polaroid. What happens to the light intensity transmitted?

3 What conclusions can you make from your experiments about the difference between light from the lamp and light transmitted by Polaroid? Explain why the first piece of Polaroid is called the polariser and say how the second Polaroid can analyse the light and detect the plane of polarisation.

4 Using *one* piece of Polaroid as an analyser, look at light from the lamp which is reflected (i) from the bench; (ii) from a sheet of glass; (iii) from a metal plate or the shining metal surfaces of a knife; (iv) from a polythene sheet.

Is there any polarisation of the reflected beam?

Does the angle at which the light is reflected have any effect on what you observe?

What kind of materials produce some polarisation at reflection? What kind does not? (The essential difference may be an electrical one since light is an electromagnetic wave.)

5 Fill the transparent tank with water to which one drop of milk has been added. The milk produces a suspension of tiny particles of fat in the water. (Too much milk would produce more than one scattering encounter for the light and the effect of scattering by single particles would not be seen.) The diagram (figure 4.19) shows where the Polaroid is placed to observe the light which is scattered through 90°. What has happened to the light scattered through 90°?

Explain, with the help of a diagram and by consulting your reference books, how you can account for your result, assuming that light waves must have an electric field vibrating across the direction of propagation.

6 In step 5 you examined the effect of a single scattering encounter. If light travels through a sheet of waxed paper it will undergo multiple scatterings and reflections. Place a small piece of waxed paper between crossed Polaroids. Say what you observe and suggest a possible explanation.

7 What evidence has been provided in steps 1 to 5 that light is a transverse wave?

Investigating stress (optional)

Apparatus

O light source
O 2 pieces of Polaroid
O transparent adhesive tape
O microscope slide
O polythene
O red filter

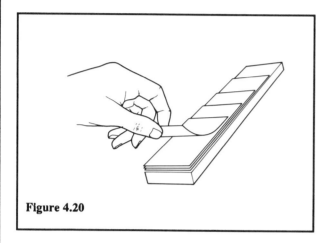

Figure 4.20

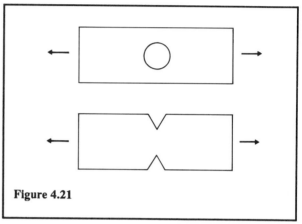

Figure 4.21

1 Set up a light source and two crossed Polaroids separated by a few centimetres. Take 10 cm of transparent adhesive tape, get a firm grip of the ends and give it a good stretch. Stick it on a microscope slide and trim the ends. View the light transmitted through the specimen when it is placed between the crossed Polaroids. Rotate the specimen and note any colour changes.

Note. The colour you see will depend on the stress in the stretched tape (a uniform colour will indicate that you have pulled it uniformly). The colour effect is produced by double refraction in the film and the speed of one of the refracted plane-polarised waves is determined by the stress in the film. The observed effect of double refraction changes with the stress and with the thicknesses of the stressed plastic. In the next section you can observe the colour sequence obtained in a stressed film of varying thickness.

2 Take about 25 cm of tape and pull it until it looks pale yellow between crossed Polaroids. Now add successive layers to the slide, building up the thickness in steps (see figure 4.20). Record the colour sequence as the thickness increases.

Note. The same colour sequence will indicate increasing stress in a film of equal thickness, and you can observe this in the following sections.

3 Tear a piece of polythene from a sheet and examine it between crossed Polaroids. (Stress has been produced by the tear which has become permanent.)

4 Observe and record the colour changes produced as you steadily stretch the polythene between crossed Polaroids. Compare the sequence with that obtained in step 2.

5 Take two strips of transparent tape. Cut notches in one and punch a hole in the other (figure 4.21). Stretch the tape, fix it on a slide, and observe the stress patterns using white light and red light. Draw a sketch showing the regions of 'stress concentration', indicated by the concentration of isochromatic (same colour) fringes.

Questions on objectives

1 Light and X-rays are both said to be electromagnetic waves.
(a) What kind of experimental results suggest that both are waves?
(b) Mention any evidence that might suggest that light and X-rays are the same kind of radiation.
(c) What arguments, based on experimental results, can you give to suggest that they have very different wavelengths?

(objectives 2 and 3)

2 Suggest reasons for
(a) the blue of the sky,
(b) the red of the sunset,
(c) the white of the clouds. *(objective 1)*

3 In a fine mist, clearer photographs of distant objects can be taken by infra-red film than by film sensitive only to visible light, yet when the fog is thick, neither film can be used. Explain. *(objective 3 and 4)*

4 Explain what is meant by plane-polarised light. Describe one method of producing a plane-polarised beam. Why is it not possible to polarise sound waves?

(objective 6)

5 An analyser for a light beam is available. How would you use it to distinguish between
(a) partially polarised,
(b) completely plane-polarised,
(c) unpolarised light? *(objective 6)*

6 Sketch a diagram showing how Polaroid sun glasses can be used to reduce glare
(a) from the surface of a river,
(b) from sunlight when the sun is vertically overhead.
Indicate on your sketch the direction in the Polaroid which transmits plane-polarised light. *(objective 6)*

TOPIC 5

Superposition

Study time: 1.5-2 weeks

Summary

This topic opens with the crucial observation in favour of the wave theory of light, and develops the theory to explain a variety of interference and diffraction effects. The importance of these in measuring both the very small and the very large is then considered. Interference also enables a two-dimensional pattern to produce a three-dimensional image in a hologram.

These holographic images show interference where a medieval painting is changing shape as a result of atmospheric changes. Why is this a useful technique?

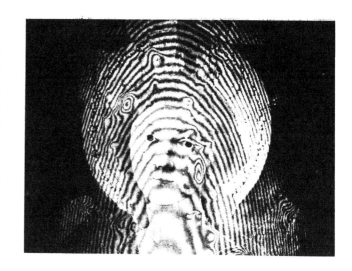

Objectives

When you have completed this topic you should be able to:

1 Use the following scientific terms correctly: diffraction, diffraction pattern, zero order image, first order maximum, transmission gratings, spectrometer, pure spectrum, emission and absorption spectra, line spectrum, continuous spectrum, monochromatic source.

2 State the conditions required to produce a steady interference pattern using light waves.

3 Perform and describe an experiment to determine the wavelength of light, using Young's method.

4 Use the expression for the wavelength in terms of slit separation s, fringe separation x and distance D from slit sources to fringe pattern,

$$\lambda = \frac{xs}{D}$$

5 Solve problems involving relationships between phase difference and path difference, including the analysis of interference patterns.

6 Describe briefly the diffraction patterns formed by a straight edge, single slit and circular aperture.

7 Describe and explain the diffraction pattern of a single slit and list the factors which influence the angular separation between central maximum and first minimum.

8 Describe and explain the main features of the pattern obtained when light passes through a diffraction grating.

9 Use the equation relating the wavelength with the angular separation of the diffracted spectra and the coarseness of the grating,

$$n\lambda = s \sin \theta$$

10 Outline an experiment to determine the wavelength of light using a transmission grating.

11 Use a Rayleigh criteria to derive resolving power, and discuss the importance of the latter in the formation of images.

12 Outline the requirements for producing a pure spectrum using (i) a prism, and (ii) a diffraction grating. Distinguish between the spectra produced in each case.

13 Describe one form of spectrometer and give an example of its use.

Experiments

WV 13 Young's double slit experiment   (1.5 hour)
WV 14 Waves through small apertures   (1.5 hour)
WV 15 Resolving power   (0.5 hour)
WV 16 Diffraction patterns   (1.5 hour)
WV 17 Observing spectra   (0.75 hour)

References

Akrill   Chapter 27
Bolton   Chapter 9
Duncan   Chapter 20
Muncaster   Chapters 25, 26 and 28
Nelkon   Chapters 19 and 20
Whelan   Chapters 35, 38, and 39

5.1 Interference

Huygens' wave theory of light predicted that wavelets would interfere when superposed, that is when they passed through the same point at the same time. The effect was not observed, however, for over one hundred years. Throughout the eighteenth century the prevailing view was that of Newton's 'corpuscles' of light.

The crucial experimental work which decided in favour of a wave theory for light was performed by Thomas Young at the beginning of the nineteenth century. His most famous experiment was the observation of fringes when light waves from the same source passed through two narrow parallel slits arranged close together. His results provided clear evidence that, under certain conditions, light plus light gave darkness. That is, destructive interference was occurring: an effect which could only be explained if light was a periodic wave. Light waves are constantly being superposed, but we only obtain a steady interference pattern under very special conditions. It required a genius like Thomas Young to realise the nature of the problem and provide a solution.

The difficulty lies not only in the very short wavelength of light, but also in the relationship between different light waves. For interference, it is necessary for the waves to be coherent.

Conditions for producing a visible interference pattern

Coherent waves have a constant phase relationship - they are said to be **phase linked**.

Q 5.1 Development question*

(a) What can you deduce about the frequencies of coherent waves?
(b) Are two dippers on the same vibrating bar coherent sources for a ripple tank?
(c) Under what conditions are two dippers on separate vibrating bars coherent?
(d) Are two flute players playing the *same* note coherent sources, and would they produce a steady sound interference pattern?
(e) What would happen to any pattern produced in (d) if one flute player stopped for breath and then started again?
(f) Are you likely to get a steady interference pattern from two flute-playing groups, even if they are all playing the same note? Explain. ■

A light source may appear to be emitting a steady wave. In fact, the light is emitted as a multitude of wave pulses. Each pulse is produced when there is an energy change in an individual atom and each lasts about 10^{-8} s or a million vibrations. Any constant phase relationship between two *separate* light sources lasts for much less than 10^{-8} s. It is, therefore, quite impossible for two separate sources of light to produce a visible interference pattern, just as no sound interference pattern would be expected from two flute bands. It is also clear that light waves from different parts of the same source will not have a constant phase relationship.

To produce a steady interference pattern, light waves must be superposed at a point after travelling by different paths. However, they should have come originally from the *same* point of the *same source* and the superposed waves must originate from the *same wavepulse*. This means that the path difference must be less than the pulse length.

Summary

1 Two coherent light sources must be derived from the same point source or slit. (The laser is an exception to this, since it produces coherent light from atoms acting in unison. Two different parts of the laser beam can be used to produce steady interference.)

2 To obtain a clear and extensive pattern, the primary source should be monochromatic. Interference patterns can be observed with white light, but are less clear because they consist of several superimposed patterns produced by different frequencies/colours.

3 The secondary sources should be very close together. This ensures that there is a region where the waves superpose, and that the fringe separation is large enough to be detected easily.

4 The interfering light waves must be unpolarised, or polarised in the same plane.

5 The coherent wavetrains should have similar amplitude.

There are two ways in which two coherent wavetrains can be produced from one source, by division of the **wavefront** or by division of the **amplitude**. In Young's experiment, coherent wavetrains are produced by division of the wavefront.

Young's double slit experiment

Figure 5.1 shows a plane perpendicular to the slits. The primary slit S is illuminated by monochromatic light. Light waves are diffracted through this slit to illuminate the second slits S_1 and S_2, which are arranged parallel to the primary slit.

Diffracted waves emerge from S_1 and S_2 and, since they originate from the same source, they have a constant phase relationship. The slits S_1 and S_2 must be very close together, so that the waves are diffracted enough to produce an area where the two waves are superposed. Interference effects can be observed anywhere in the region where superposition occurs, so there are many possible positions for the screen.

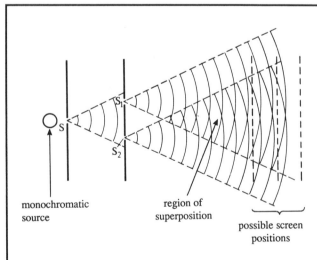

monochromatic source

region of superposition

possible screen positions

Figure 5.1

E Experiment WV 13
Young's double slit experiment

You will replicate Young's experiment to produce an interference pattern from two slits, and measure the wavelength of light.

Figure 5.2 indicates the geometry of a Young's double slit experiment. S_1 and S_2 represent coherent sources, in phase, and OM is the perpendicular bisector of S_1S_2. The diagram is *not* drawn to scale since, in this experiment, S_1S_2 is less than 1 mm, OM is about 1 m and OP is a few millimetres. There will be constructive interference at all points along line OM, because the path difference along this line is zero. At point O on the screen there will be maximum light (the zero order maximum). To find the effect at any other point P on the screen we must find the path difference at P.

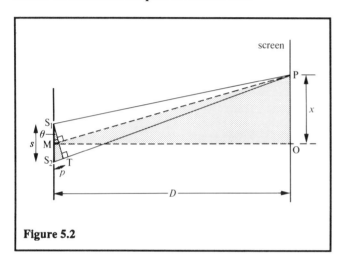

Figure 5.2

(d) If the $(n + 1)$th bright fringe is at a distance x_{n+1} from O, what is x_{n+1} in terms of λ?
(e) What is the separation between the nth and the $(n + 1)$th bright fringes?
(f) Explain why the pattern on the screen looks like figure 5.3. ∎

A double slit interference pattern for monochromatic light consists of equally spaced bright and dark fringes, parallel to slits. They can be seen on a screen, or in an eyepiece, anywhere in the region where the waves are superposed (figure 5.1).

From an interference pattern similar to that shown in figure 5.3, the wavelength of light from a monochromatic source can be calculated, using

$$\text{wavelength} = \frac{\text{slit separation} \times \text{fringe separation}}{\text{distance from slits to fringes}}$$

$$\lambda = \frac{sx}{D}, \text{ if } D \gg s$$

Figure 5.3

Q 5.2 Development question*

(a) T is a point on the line S_2P such that $PT = PS_1$. What does the length TS_2 represent (note that it is equal to $PS_2 - PS_1$)?
(b) M is the midpoint of S_1S_2. Assuming that PM bisects line S_1T, why is PM perpendicular to S_1T?
(c) If the line S_1T is rotated through an angle θ, so that it lies along S_1S_2, where will line MP be?
(d) What is the value of the angle PMO?
(e) Why is angle S_1TS_2 almost equal to 90°?
(f) What does this imply about triangle TS_1S_2 and triangle OMP?
(g) From part (f), $TS_2/S_1S_2 = OP/PM$. Show how this leads to the equation $p = sx/D$.
(h) Some approximations have been made in obtaining this result. Why are these approximations justified? ∎

Q 5.3 Development question*

(a) The zero order bright fringe is at O. The first bright fringe is at a distance x_1 from O. What is the path difference for this fringe? Write an equation relating λ and x_1.
(b) If the second bright fringe is at a distance x_2 from O, write an equation relating λ and x_2.
(c) If the nth bright fringe is at a distance x_n from O, what is x_n in terms of λ ?

Q 5.4 Self-assessment question

A double slit interference pattern is produced using a monochromatic slit source and two slits 1.0 mm apart. The fringes are seen 1.20 m from the double slit. If the distance across twenty fringes is 14.2 mm, what is the wavelength of light from the source?

Q 5.5 Self-assessment question

The equation $x = \lambda D/s$ is derived by assuming that D is very much larger than s. It is a useful approximate relationship, even when applied to the interference pattern in a ripple tank. From figure 5.18a (see page 86) calculate the wavelength from the interference pattern, using the formula, and compare this value with a direct measurement of wavelength from the photograph. ∎

When observing a double slit interference pattern one can locate the minima more precisely than the maxima. The separation of adjacent minima is the same as the separation of adjacent maxima.

How bright is the screen at places between a maximum and a minimum? At these points the superposing waves are neither in phase nor completely out of phase.

The amplitude of the resultant wave varies between maximum and minimum like a sine or cosine curve, so the brightness along the screen (which depends on the square of the amplitude) varies like a graph of $\cos^2\theta$, with a zero order maximum at the midpoint O of the pattern. Figure 5.4 shows a graph of relative light intensity I/I_0 against distance x along the screen from O when monochromatic light passes through two very narrow slits.

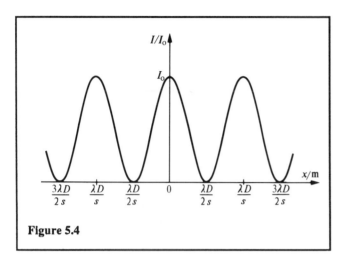

Figure 5.4

The theory outlined above assumes that the sources S_1 and S_2 are slits of negligible width, producing many equally bright fringes. Figure 5.3 shows that, although the fringes are equidistant, they are not equally bright. This is because the slits have a finite width.

The slit width is significant, because wavelets travelling to a point from different parts of the same slit do not have the same phase. This fact limits the number of bright fringes seen in the pattern. Wider slits give fewer fringes, and not all fringes are equally bright. You are, in fact, observing a double slit diffraction pattern, which will be studied in the next section. In the following questions you can assume that the slits have negligible width.

Q 5.6 Self-assessment question

In a Young's slit experiment the slits are 5.0×10^{-4} m apart and the distance between the slits and the screen is 2.0 m. The experiment is performed using a white light source, first with a filter which passes only blue light ($\lambda = 4.5 \times 10^{-7}$ m) and then with a filter passing only yellow light ($\lambda = 6.0 \times 10^{-7}$ m).

(a) What is the fringe spacing in each case?

(b) Sketch graphs, on the same axes, showing how the light intensity varies with distance along the screen for blue light and for yellow light. Each graph should extend from the central maximum to the fourth bright fringe on one side of the centre.

(c) A filter which passes only blue light and yellow light, in equal intensities, is placed in front of the source. A black and white film is placed in the position of the screen. Using the data provided by your calculations and graphs, sketch a further graph to show how the blackening of the film will vary with distance from the centre of the pattern when the film is developed (assuming that blackening is proportional to the light intensity reaching the film). ∎

White light fringes

Young's original experiments were performed with white light. Let us analyse this kind of pattern by considering how the light intensity varies for particular colours of the spectrum.

Q 5.7 Development question*

(a) Sketch a graph (similar to figure 5.4) showing how the intensity will vary for blue light passing through a double slit, from the first minimum on one side to the third minimum on the other side of the centre.
(b) On the same diagram, sketch the intensity curve for red light passing through the same double slit. (Assume that $\lambda_{red}/\lambda_{blue} = 3/2$ and that the sources have the same intensity.)
(c) At which point on the screen is there always a maximum intensity for all colours? Explain this.
(d) Describe the appearance of the zero order bright fringe when a white light source is used.
(e) Describe the appearance of the first order bright fringe, saying how it differs from the central fringe.
(f) Will there be a minimum between the first and second bright fringes?
(g) Estimate the maximum number of fringes you are likely to observe with white light, and explain your estimate. ∎

You can view white light fringes formed by two slits using the double slits prepared for experiment WV13. Hold the double slit close to your eye and view a distant line filament lamp. When Young's fringes are viewed with white light it is easy to locate the central (zero order) maximum, because the central fringe is different from the rest. This makes it easier to locate any movement in the fringe pattern.

Q 5.8 Self-assessment question

The arrangement in figure 5.5 produces white light fringes on a screen.

(a) What change in the pattern will be observed if the slit S is moved in the direction of the arrow?
(b) What will happen if, with S in its original position, the double slits are moved in the same direction?
(c) Will any changes in the brightness or spacing of the fringes be observed if slit S is moved towards the double slits? Can S be too near to the double slits? Suggest reasons, remembering that S_1 and S_2 are illuminated by light diffracted through S. ∎

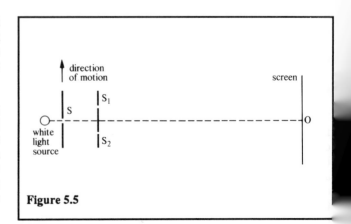

Figure 5.5

Q 5.9 Study question

Try to investigate the interference of v.h.f. radio or TV waves due to reflection from a metal sheet or large metal fence (tennis court fencing). The published table of v.h.f. radio transmitters will tell you in which direction the waves reach you.

Place the portable v.h.f. radio between the station and the reflector (figure 5.6) and move it slowly perpendicular to the reflector. The rod aerial can be used or, better still, a special v.h.f. aerial. The best sets have circuits designed to keep the output volume constant, so a cheap radio is more suitable for this experiment and should be tuned slightly 'off station'. You can try the effect with u.h.f. television signals by moving an aerial perpendicular to a metal plate.

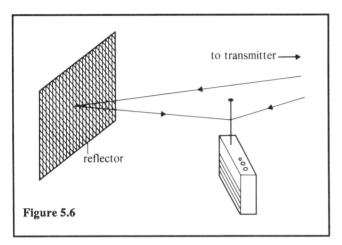

Figure 5.6

Use the method to obtain a measurement of the wavelength of the radio waves and compare this with the calibrated wavelength or frequency on your dial. ■

5.2 Diffraction

In experiment WV2 you observed how ripples spread out around an obstacle, or after passing through a small gap (figure 5.7). **Diffraction** is the term used to describe this effect, and it is a property of all waves. We take for granted the diffraction of sound waves which spread around obstacles and round the corners of gaps, like doorways. Equally, we accept that we cannot *see* around corners. Sound and light behave differently, yet we have evidence that sound and light are both waves and share wave properties. When we compare their wavelengths, it is not really surprising that they behave very differently.

Q 5.10 Self-assessment question

Compare the wavelength of a sound wave of frequency 170 Hz with that of light of average wavelength 5×10^{-7} m (speed of sound = 340 m s^{-1}). ■

Things appear a different size to sound waves and to light. It is obvious that if we are to observe any bending of light round obstacles or through gaps, we will have to go out of our way by looking for diffraction effects using very tiny apertures and obstacles. If diffraction effects occur in light, it is obviously of some significance because everything we see of the world is due to light passing through a small hole, the pupil of our eye.

Q 5.11 Self-assessment question

Figure 5.7 shows the diffraction effects produced when water waves of different wavelengths pass through different gaps. Figure 5.7a, b and c illustrate the same wavelength. Comment on the important features of each pattern and suggest what factor makes them different. State any agreement you have found in your experiment between the behaviour of light waves and ripples. ■

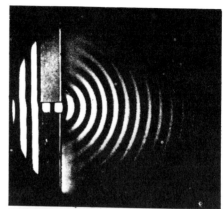

(a)

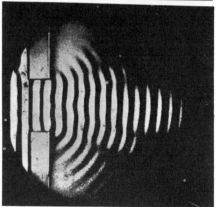

(b)

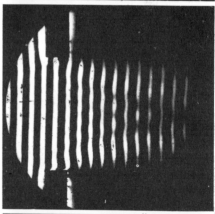

(c)

(d)

Figure 5.7

Q 5.12 Self-assessment question

(a) If you wanted to carry out an experiment for observing the diffraction of sound waves at a slit, what kind of sound source would you use? How would you detect the sound diffracted, and what size of slit would you use?

(b) If you live some distance from a building housing a disco, you will almost certainly hear the music even though there are houses between you and the disco! Why does this happen? The low bass notes will be much more audible than other sounds. Suggest a possible explanation of this effect. ∎

Defining diffraction

E Experiment WV 14
Waves through small apertures

You will set up an arrangement to enable you to see diffraction patterns caused by light passing through small holes.

A series of single slit diffraction patterns are shown in figure 5.8. These were obtained by varying the width of the slit while keeping the wavelength of the light constant. Two obvious features of the single slit diffraction pattern are:

1 The light waves extend into the region which would be in shadow if light travelled in straight lines.

2 Inside the shadow the light intensity varies, producing faint fringes.

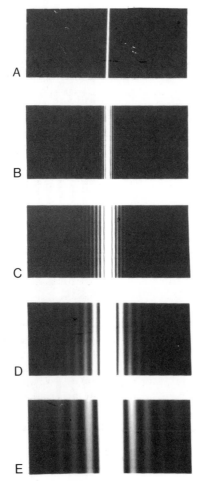

Figure 5.8

You have already observed the interference fringes produced by superposition of waves from two coherent sources. The presence of bright and dark fringes in the single slit diffraction patterns (figure 5.8) suggests that perhaps even in this case we are observing an effect of superposition of wave energies. How can this be possible when we are only dealing with one wave from one aperture? It is true that there is only one aperture, but wave energy reaching the screen is coming from different parts of the aperture and these separate energy sources combine to produce the observed diffraction effect.

A diffraction pattern is defined as the effect produced when waves from sources on the same wave front are superposed after the wavefront has been restricted by an obstacle or aperture.

Q 5.13 Development question*

(a) What property of two waves should be added together when the waves are superposed?

(b) How can the resulting amplitude be found when two waves of the same frequency but different phases are superposed?

(c) The intensity of light is defined as the rate at which light energy is radiated through unit area. What relationship relates intensity and amplitude for a light wave? ∎

When light waves from different sources on the same wavefront are superposed, it is the wave amplitudes at particular points which must be added together (vectorially) but the results of this superposition are observed as a variation in light intensity which we call a diffraction pattern.

To predict the light intensity distribution produced by diffraction, Huygens' principle is applied. Before analysing diffraction at any slit, consider what happens at a very narrow slit.

Q 5.14 Self-assessment question

(a) Does any energy travel in the direction of the arrow (figure 5.9)? Justify your answer by sketching the wavefronts to the right of the slit and marking the directions in which energy is transmitted.

(b) What would happen if the barrier were removed? How does Huygens' principle support your answer? ∎

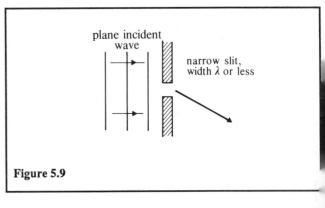

Figure 5.9

When a plane wave is diffracted at a very narrow slit (with a width of the order of a wavelength) we observe that a cylindrical diffracted wave spreads the energy out over a very large angle. To find out what happens at wider slits we can divide a wide slit into a number of narrow equal-width strips

Each strip can be considered as a very narrow slit radiating a cylindrical wave. The diffraction effect due to a wider slit can then be predicted by superimposing all these waves.

Q 5.15 Development question*

In this question we consider the wave energy diffracted *in a particular direction* making angle θ with a straight-through direction when a *plane wave* is incident at a slit. You will find the value of θ at which minimum brightness occurs.

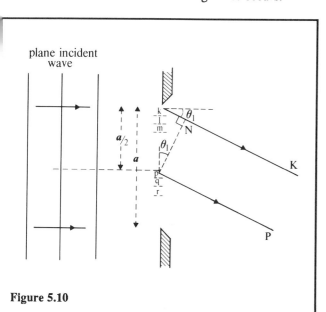

Figure 5.10

(a) The plane wavefront reaching the aperture (figure 5.10) is divided into many pairs of equal width strips each radiating waves: k and p are such a pair. Strip k is at one edge of the slit and strip p is just below the mid-point. What is the distance between k and p, l and q, and m and r?
(b) If energy travels from the slit at an angle θ_1 to the original direction, express the path difference in terms of a and θ_1 for waves from k and p travelling in directions kK and pP.
(c) For this particular angle θ_1 the path difference for waves from k and p is $\lambda/2$. What will be the effect on a distant screen where waves from k and p combine after travelling at angle θ with the original wave direction?
(d) What will be the effect on the screen for waves from l and q travelling in the same direction?
(e) The effect of light from the whole slit can be found by adding up the effects due to all the pairs of narrow strips, each $a/2$ apart. What will be the resulting effect on the screen produced by a wave diffracted in this direction?
(f) We have considered one particular value of diffracting angle θ_1 which produces zero light on the screen. Write down an expression linking λ, a and θ_1.
(g) Give reasons for thinking that at all angles less than θ_1 there will be some light reaching the screen beyond the slit.
(h) Suppose light travelling from pairs of strips $a/4$ apart has a path difference $\lambda/2$ at an angle θ_2. Predict the effect produced by waves diffracted through θ_2, and give a relationship between θ_2, a and λ.
(i) Write down an equation predicting another direction θ_3 of the diffracted waves which produces a minimum. ■

We can summarise our argument by stating that the angle between the centre of the pattern and the position of the first minimum is given by $\sin \theta_1 = \lambda/a$. This angle is important

because it tells us the angular spread ($2\theta_1$) which contains most of the energy of the wave.

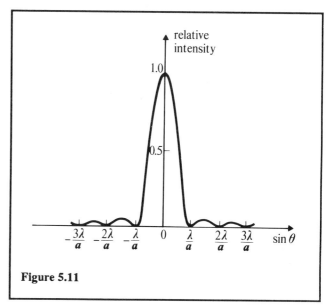

Figure 5.11

Figure 5.11 shows how the light intensity varies in different directions and emphasises that most of the energy in the diffraction pattern from a single slit is contained within the region of the central maximum. Note that the horizontal axis shows sin θ, but since the angles are very small this is almost identical to θ (in radians).

Q 5.16 Self-assessment question

(a) If the width of the slit is large compared with the wavelength, what can you say about the angular spread of the central maximum? In which direction does the light travel after passing through the slit?
(b) If the slit width is equal to (i) 3λ, and (ii) λ, what is the angular spread of the central maximum in each case?
(c) (i) What happens as the slit width is made progressively smaller than λ? (ii) How could this effect be observed? ■

Q 5.17 Self-assessment question

Sketch a possible shape for the graph of light intensity against sin θ for a slit of width λ. ■

Q 5.18 Self-assessment question

Figure 5.8 shows how the diffraction pattern changes as the width of the slit changes.

(a) Which pattern is produced by the narrowest slit?
(b) What sort of slit, if any, is used in figure 5.8a?
(c) If figure 5.8c is obtained using a slit of width 4λ, estimate the width of the slit in figure 5.8d.
(d) Do the relative widths of the central and other fringes in figure 5.8 agree with the graph in figure 5.11? ■

It is useful to divide diffraction effects into two groups:

1 Fraunhöfer diffraction patterns (figure 5.12a) are produced by the diffraction of plane waves. In question 5.14 we analysed a Fraunhöfer single slit diffraction pattern since we assumed that plane waves were incident at the slit and we considered the resulting diffraction effect in a particular

direction. Fraunhöfer diffraction is obtained when source and screen are a long way from the aperture or lenses are used.

2 Fresnel diffraction patterns (figure 5.12b) are produced when source and observer are finite distances from the obstacle or aperture. The analysis of these effects is very complex and will not be considered in this course.

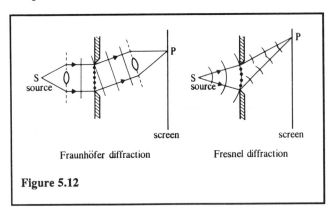

Fraunhöfer diffraction   Fresnel diffraction

Figure 5.12

In Young's double slit experiment light is diffracted through two narrow slits and a double slit interference pattern is observed where the central maximum of each diffracted wave overlaps.

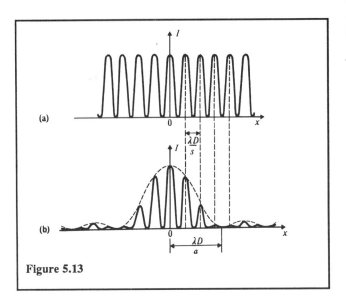

Figure 5.13

In experiment WV 13 it was assumed the slits had negligible width so that the variation in intensity would be as shown in figure 5.13a. In fact, because of the finite width a of the slits, the waves diffracted through the slits have an amplitude which varies with the angle of diffraction and the intensity curve for Young's slits is as shown in figure 5.13b. The separation of the interference fringes depends on the slit separation s while the width of the diffraction pattern depends on the width of the slits.

Q 5.19 Self-assessment question

A student rules a double slit on a painted glass slide but fails to observe Young's interference fringes. What advice would you give him for making double slits which would give a pattern bright enough to observe? Would you advise him to

(a) make the slits wider,
(b) make the slits narrow,
(c) rule the slits closer together?

Give reasons for the advice you give. ∎

5.3 Resolving power

Light through a hole, like our eye or a telescope, doesn't usually come from just one place. We observe patterns of stars, or the fine print in a book, and we want to see as much detail as possible. What effect has diffraction on the ability to see detail - to distinguish light from different places? This section will provide an answer to this question.

When you look at a row of bright filaments through a slit it is not always possible to see a row of separate sources. You are actually observing not a series of filaments but a series of diffraction patterns which may overlap so much that you cannot separate them. In this case we say the images are not resolved.

E Experiment WV 15
Resolving power

You will observe a number of light sources, and find that what you see depends on the size of the hole you look through, and the colour of the light source.

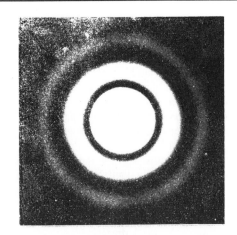

(a)

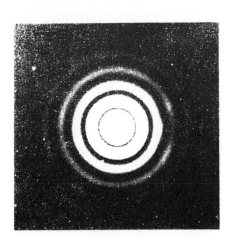

(b)

Figure 5.14

A point source viewed through a small circular aperture gives a circular diffraction pattern (figure 5.14). The size of the pattern depends on the ratio λ/D (D = diameter of aperture).

Figure 5.15 shows a point source and three pairs of point sources viewed through three different circular apertures. In (a) the opening is such that all three pairs of points are clearly resolved. Decreasing the size of the aperture increases the size of the diffraction pattern. In (b) the two upper pairs of points are clearly resolved whereas the lowest pair is near the limit of resolution.

In (c) the lowest pair are not resolved, the middle pair are near the limit of resolution and the upper pair are still clearly resolved.

Figure 5.16 shows the overlapping intensities of two images which are just resolved. The eye responds to the intensity variation curve C, the sum of A and B.

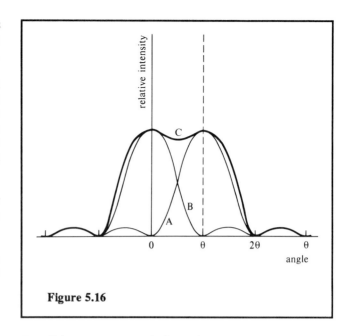

Figure 5.16

For all the apertures we shall consider D is much bigger than λ and so $\sin \theta$ is very small and can be approximated to θ. In calculations on optical instruments you can simplify the expression further and use

$$\theta \approx \frac{\text{wavelength}}{\text{diameter}}$$

where θ is the angular separation between the centre and the first dark fringe.

Q 5.20 Study question

Explain what is meant by Rayleigh's criterion for resolution illustrating your answer by appropriate light intensity graphs. Show how this leads to a way of assessing the resolving power of a telescope. ■

Q 5.21 Self-assessment question

Why do you think astronomers photograph stars through a blue filter? ■

5.4 Gratings

In the last section you observed the diffraction pattern produced by a single slit, whilst in section 5.1 you observed the interference pattern produced when light passed through two slits. What is the difference between an interference pattern and a diffraction pattern? None really! For historical reasons, the pattern produced by superposing waves from two or more separate coherent sources is usually called an **interference** pattern. The variation of intensity produced by superposing light from different parts of a continuous wave which has been obstructed is called **diffraction**. So we speak of the **interference** pattern produced by two vibrating dippers in a ripple tank, and the **diffraction** pattern from a single slit. An obstruction with many slits is called a **diffraction grating**.

Q 5.22 Study question

Figure 5.13b shows the intensity graph produced when a plane wave is diffracted by two slits.

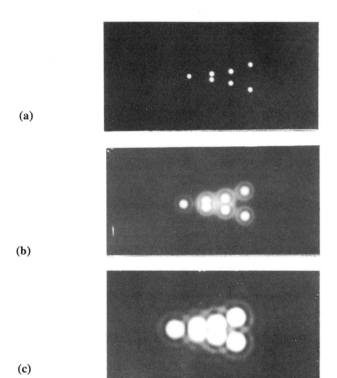

(a)

(b)

(c)

Figure 5.15

This means that optical instruments like microscopes, telescopes and eyes cannot produce a point image of a point object but only a diffraction pattern. The angular spread θ from the centre of this pattern to the first dark ring is given by the equation

$$\sin \theta = \frac{1.22\lambda}{D}$$

where λ is the wavelength of light and D is the diameter of the circular aperture.

Now study intensity graphs or photographs in your reference texts of diffraction patterns for three or more equidistant slits. Comment briefly on how an increase in the number of slits affects

(a) the spacing of the maxima,
(b) the sharpness of the maxima. ∎

Diffraction of a plane wave incident at a narrow slit produces cylindrical waves which we could draw as circles. A whole series of narrow slits would produce a set of overlapping cylindrical waves. Figure 5.17 shows the interfering waves from a series of point sources (or narrow slits).

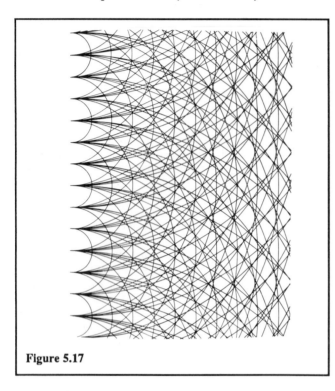

Figure 5.17

Look obliquely along the diagram (figure 5.17) from the bottom edge. Can you see some strong wavefronts travelling across the page parallel to the line of slits (figure 5.18a)?

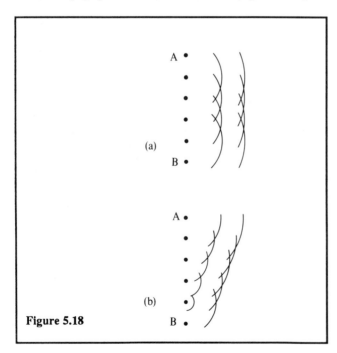

(a)

(b)

Figure 5.18

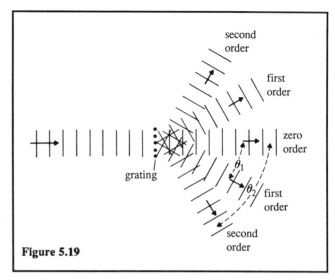

Figure 5.19

This suggests that diffraction will produce some strong undeviated waves which we will call **zero order** waves.

Turn the diagram round a little and observe a series of strong wavefronts travelling slightly oblique to AB (figure 5.18b). We can call this set a **first order** set.

Turn the book further and other more oblique strong wavefronts can be observed diffracted on both sides of the central zero order waves.

A transmission diffraction grating allows light waves to pass through a series of equidistant fine slits and produces a series of diffracted maxima (figure 5.19).

E Experiment WV 16
Diffraction patterns

In this experiment you will observe the patterns produced by fine and coarse gratings and use a fine grating to measure the wavelength of light.

Q 5.23 Study question

(a) Using figure 5.20 and considering the superposition of waves from adjacent slits, deduce a relationship between the slit separation s in a grating, the wavelength λ of the light and the angle θ_1 through which the intense first order waves are diffracted.

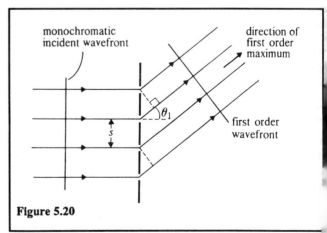

Figure 5.20

(b) What equation will link θ_2, λ and s for the second order maxima?
(c) Write down a general equation for the mth order maxima. ■

Q 5.24 Self-assessment question

Measure angles θ_1 and θ_2, s and λ for the circular waves in figure 5.19 and check whether the equations you have deduced agree with your observations of this diagram. ■

Q 5.25 Self-assessment question

Figure 5.21 shows the intensity graph for a diffraction grating illuminated normally by monochromatic light. The sharp peaks of the pattern of superposition are enclosed within the diffraction envelope produced by each slit.

(a) If the grating has 6000 lines per cm, calculate the wavelength of the light.
(b) Will third order maxima be visible? Explain.
(c) Estimate from the graph the width of each slit in the grating. ■

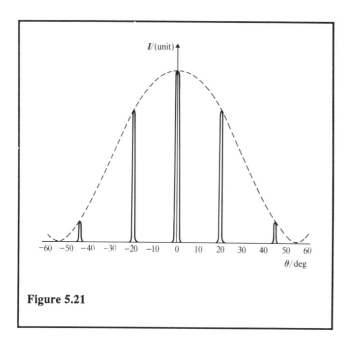

Figure 5.21

Q 5.26 Self-assessment question

A gramophone record will act as a reflection grating. To observe the effect, the reflection of a distant fluorescent tube lamp must be viewed very obliquely in the record. Why do you think the pattern is only seen when viewed obliquely? Which direction must the fluorescent tube point in for the best results? Draw a sketch and try the experiment if you can find time. ■

Q 5.27 Self-assessment question

A distant sodium street lamp is viewed through a piece of muslin and two sets of five equally spaced lamps are seen in rows, each row at right angles to one set of the threads of the material.
The outermost lamps appear to be separated by an angle of 0.01 radian. Estimate the number of threads in a metre of the material, assuming the wavelength of light is 6×10^{-7} m. ■

C Comprehension WV 3
Diffraction rules the waves

An ingenious idea to tap wave energy by a sea-side diffraction grating.

5.5 Spectra

How is it possible to find out what kind of light is being emitted by a source? Our eye responds to a range of waves whose wavelengths in air vary between about 4×10^{-7} m and 7×10^{-7} m. Through our eyes we receive the total message - the summed up effect of all the different component wavelengths in the light which gives the source its particular colour and brightness. But if we want to identify the different components present in the light we need to be able to separate them. The diffraction grating provides us with a very convenient 'separator'.

You have looked at a light source through a diffraction grating and will have observed that (except for the zero order beam) the angle at which the light is diffracted strongly depends on its wavelength. A source emitting several wavelengths produces diffracted beams which are separated into component wavelengths. This separation of light into component colours is an example of **dispersion**.

A rainbow is formed by dispersion when light from the sun is refracted and reflected internally by raindrops. Isaac Newton studied the dispersion of light by a prism and later Joseph Fraunhöfer began to develop simple gratings in order to observe dispersion effects. The band of colour produced by dispersion is an example of a **spectrum**. It is really a series of different coloured images of the source.

E Experiment WV 17
Observing spectra

In this investigation you will compare the spectra of different light sources and note the differences between spectra produced by a grating and a prism.

The spectrometer

To analyse light effectively we need to produce a pure spectrum and also obtain a lot of dispersion so that very close wavelengths can be separated or resolved. A **pure spectrum** is produced when there is no overlapping of colours because every component wavelength produces a separate image of the slit. A spectrometer is an instrument for producing and measuring pure spectra. (Figure 5.22)

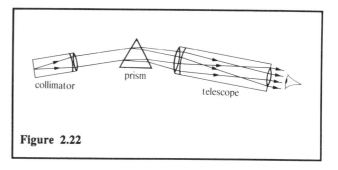

Figure 2.22

Light from the collimator passes through the prism, and the resulting spectrum can be examined through the telescope. The spectrometer is fitted with an angular scale so that the angle between the collimator and telescope can be measured, and we shall be concerned here with its use in an accurate method for measuring the refractive index of glass for a particular wavelength of light.

Q 5.28 Study question*

Think what components you would need to obtain a good spectrum - as close as possible to 'pure'. Study your books to find how a pure spectrum is produced.
(a) List the apparatus needed to produce a pure spectrum.
(b) State the function of each component.
(c) Show by a diagram how they should be arranged. (Check your list with the answer provided.) ■

Q 5.29 Study question

(a) Describe how you would use a spectrometer to measure the angle of a prism and the angle of minimum deviation. State what measurements you would take and how you would use them to find the refractive index of the material of the prism.
(b) Describe a method for measuring the wavelength of light from a sodium lamp using a diffraction grating and a spectrometer. Outline the adjustment of the spectrometer and state what readings are taken in measuring the results. ■

If a spectrometer is available, set up and adjust the spectrometer for yourself and measure the refractive index of the glass of a prism for sodium light. (The same method can be used to measure the refractive index of a liquid. The liquid is enclosed in a hollow glass prism.)

Q 5.30 Self-assessment question

Can you suggest any reasons why a grating is often preferred to a prism in modern spectrometers? ■

Types of spectra

How can we classify spectra? The light from a glowing substance produces an **emission spectrum**. When white light passes through an absorbing medium like a coloured filter an **absorption spectrum** of the material is produced. This absorption can also occur in liquids and gases and can occur even when the gas is glowing.

A study of how spectra are produced leads to important theories about atomic structure which are discussed in the unit *Electrons and the nucleus*.

Q 5.31 Study question

Make notes on how spectra are classified into line, band and continuous spectra, indicating why the different names are appropriate and stating what kinds of sources produce each type. ■

We know from the type of emission or absorption spectrum produced whether the light has been emitted or absorbed by atomic vapours, molecular vapours, liquids or solids. Much more significantly, the uniqueness of each line or band spectrum indicates that the light has been emitted or absorbed by a particular element or compound. This study of spectra provides a versatile technique for analysing substances. By using photographic or photocell detectors, which are extremely sensitive, the method can detect and measure the proportion of an element present in a mixture to one part in a million. The spectrum of the incandescent vapour of the substance being analysed can be obtained using a metal or carbon arc lamp or a discharge tube. Substances may also be analysed from their absorption spectra and this method is particularly important for biological material or foodstuffs. Many of the important characteristic lines are in the ultraviolet region, whilst infra-red spectra are important in learning about the bonding and structure of complex molecules.

C Comprehension WV 4
Spectroscopy at work

This article describes applications of spectroscopy to steelmaking (ultraviolet), chemical research (visible) and molecular analysis (infra-red).

Young's double slit experiment

Apparatus

○ vertical filament lamp (12 V, 36 W) with stand and shield
○ microscope slide
○ slide holder for ruling slits
○ Aquadag
○ needle

○ translucent screen
○ adjustable slit
○ eyepiece (magnifying glass) and holder
○ green filter
○ transparent millimetre scale
○ leads
○ metre rule

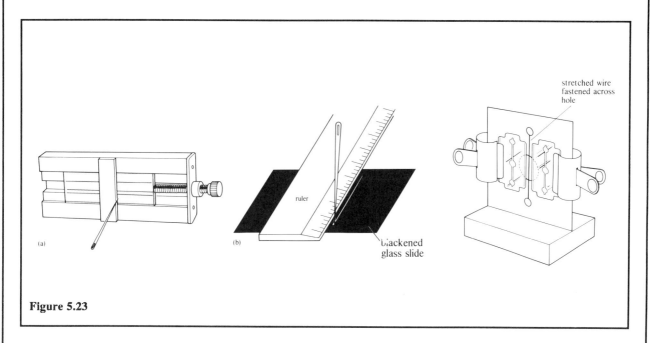

Figure 5.23

In this experiment you have to make your own apparatus for obtaining Young's fringes and measuring the average wavelength of light which passes through a green filter. Setting up the apparatus successfully requires an unusual amount of patience and care, which will be rewarded by obtaining an impressive pattern. These experimental notes are not a step-by-step recipe to obtain fringes, but a series of notes on the experimental set-up. Sometimes, alternative approaches are indicated. Read right through the notes and then decide on your own strategy.

1 Constructing a double slit

(a) The double slit can be ruled on a microscope slide which has been coated with colloidal graphite (Aquadag). Ideally, the slide should be coated a few hours before ruling so that the coating is hard. The coating should be opaque, but not too thick. The slide can be placed in a special holder (figure 5.23a), and one slit ruled with a blunt needle or razor blade. Then the screw, with a pitch of 0.5 mm, is used to displace the slide so that a second slit can be ruled.

Figure 5.23b shows an alternative method of ruling the lines which requires more skill. The slits should not be more than 0.55 mm apart (centre-to-centre). Try to make the two slits of equal width. Wide slits produce a brighter pattern, but few fringes.

The widest slit allowable, for a reasonable pattern, will be of width equal to half the slit separation (i.e. slits of width x with an opaque region of width x between them). Several pairs of slits can be ruled on the same slide, and tested by holding the slide to your eye and looking at a distance line filament lamp. This will enable you to judge brightness, definition and separation for fringes produced by different double slits.

(b) An alternative arrangement for producing a double slit is shown in figure 5.23c. A length of bare copper wire, s.w.g. 26, is stretched until it gives. A piece of this wire is glued across a hole in a piece of tin plate. The positions of the razor blades are adjusted to produce two narrow slits of equal width.

continued

EXPERIMENT WV 13

2 Making a slit source

The source is a lamp with a vertical line filament. A shield around the lamp prevents stray light reaching the screen. An adjustable slit, formed between two razor blades, should be placed in front of the filament lamp to increase the definition of the pattern.

3 Arranging the apparatus

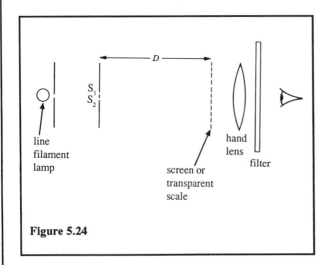

Figure 5.24

Make sure the lamp, slits and viewing screen (or lens) are in line, and that the filament and all the slits are parallel to each other (figure 5.24). The distance from the source to the double slits should be about 1 metre.

The distance D from the double slits to the screen determines the separation of the fringes. It must be two or more metres when the slit separation is 0.5 mm, but if the slits are closer together the viewing distance can be less. If a lens is used to magnify the pattern, the distance D can be reduced to as little as 30 cm. When the fringes are clearly visible, hold a green filter in front of your eye. Two factors which may prevent you obtaining a good pattern are (i) having slit S too wide, and (ii) making slits S_1 and S_2 unequal in width. Take care to eliminate these factors.

4 Viewing the pattern

A translucent screen can be used to view the fringes. Alternatively, a magnifying glass or microscope eyepiece can be used to view fringes located just in front of the lens, in the object plane. Stray light can be reduced by placing the screen at the end of a box or long tube blackened on the inside. (A travelling microscope with the objective lens removed provides a viewing lens and a tube to reduce stray light.)

5 Taking measurements

(a) The fringe separation x (the distance from the centre of one dark fringe to the centre of the next dark fringe) can be found by (i) marking on the screen the location of the dark fringes at the edges of the pattern, (ii) placing the transparent scale in front of the viewing lens, so that the scale divisions are in sharp focus and superimposed on the fringe pattern formed in the same plane as the scale. Alternatively, a travelling microscope can be used.

(b) The slit separation can be found by (i) placing the transparent scale across or alongside the slide and looking at the slits and the scale through a magnifying glass or microscope, or (ii) using a travelling microscope, or (iii) placing the lamp just behind the double slits and using a lens to obtain a magnified image of the slits on the screen.

6 Calculating the wavelength

The wavelength λ of the light forming the fringes is given by the equation $\lambda = sx/D$, where s is the slit separation, x the fringe separation and D the distance from slits to fringes. Obtain a value for the average wavelength transmitted by the filter. State briefly how you measured each of the quantities in the above equation, and estimate the possible percentage error in each quantity. (Section 2.4 of the *Student's resource book* is about estimating experimental errors.) Write down your answer for the value of wavelength λ, stating the estimated experimental error and giving the correct number of significant figures.

EXPERIMENT WV 14

Waves through small apertures

Apparatus

○ 12 V, 24 W line filament lamp
○ SBC holder
○ 12 V a.c. supply
○ translucent screen
○ lens, converging, $f = 50$ cm
○ filters (red and green)
○ metal foil
○ copper wire, 36 s.w.g.
○ 2 razor blades
○ scissors
○ rubber bands
○ cardboard
○ (optional) adjustable slit , screw controlled

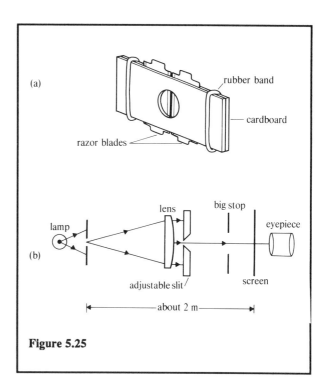

Figure 5.25

1 Make a very small hole in a piece of aluminium foil. A suitable size for the hole is obtained by using copper wire, 36 s.w.g. First stretch the copper until it breaks and then hold one of the broken ends in between your fingers a few mm from the end and pierce the foil firmly. Hold the pin hole to your eye and look at a 'point source' of light 3 m away in a darkened room. What do you observe?

Note. A 'point source' is an idealised source, to which a bulb with a small filament or a line filament approximates when it illuminates a small hole in a screen placed in front of the lamp.

2 View the source through slightly larger pin holes made using a pin or thicker wire. Does the source of light look smaller when the hole is smaller? Describe the changes you observe for different size holes.

3 Make a narrow slit between the edges of two razor blades as shown in figure 5.25a. Look at the slit against an illuminated background like a window and adjust the blades so that the edges form as narrow and parallel-sided a slit as possible. In a darkened room, view a line filament lamp through the narrow slit held near your eye, parallel to the filament and at least 3 m from it. Do your observations through holes and slits support the idea of the wave theory of light? Give a reason for your answer.

4 The use of a lens will enable diffraction effects to be observed on a screen. Arrange the apparatus as shown in figure 5.25b but without the adjustable slit. Place the lens midway between the lamp and screen which are just over 2 m apart. Place a vertical slit in front of the lamp and parallel to the filament. Move the screen until an image of the slit is focused on the screen.

Place the adjustable slit near to the lens and parallel to the slit source and observe the pattern on the screen. A big stop (a card with 2 cm diameter hole) provides a way of cutting out light which has not passed through the slit and the best position for it must be found by trial and error. Observe the pattern produced on the screen when light passes through a fine slit.

5 Record how the pattern changes as the slit width changes. The pattern can be seen in more detail if a lower power eyepiece is used. The eyepiece can be moved so that it is focused on the translucent screen and then the screen can be removed and fine focusing of the eyepiece completed. The lamp may have to be adjusted so that light falls centrally on the eyepiece lens.

6 Place first a red and then a green filter in front of the light source, and say how the pattern changes.

Note: If you have difficulty in obtaining a pattern on the screen check

(a) that light from the source is falling on the adjustable slit (move the source slit if necessary),
(b) that light from the slit source is entering the eyepiece (check this by removing the adjustable slit and holding a card in front of the eyepiece).

Resolving power

Apparatus

○ multiple light source
○ narrow slit
○ red, green and blue filters
○ white card

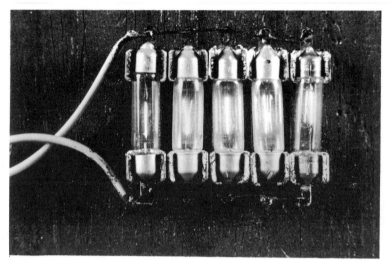

Figure 5.26

Viewing through a slit

1 Cover the multiple light source (figure 5.26) with a green filter and look at it through a narrow slit 3 m from the lamp. Adjust the width of the slit until the lamp can just be seen as separate lights and not as a continuous strip.

2 Without changing the slit width or your viewing position, observe the effect when the green filter is replaced by a blue filter and then a red one. Comment on your results.

Resolving detail with the eye

1 Rule two black parallel lines 2 mm apart on a white card. Illuminate the card well. Find the greatest distance at which you can distinguish the two black lines.

2 Calculate the angular separation between two objects which you can just resolve. Compare your results with others in the group and comment on any differences.

92

Unit WV
Superposition

Diffraction patterns

Apparatus

○ coarse grating, approx. 1000 lines per cm
○ fine grating, approx. 6000 lines per cm
○ line filament lamp and holder
○ metre rule
○ red filter

Note: The grating you will use is a tranmission grating which uses a thin plastic sheet whose surface is moulded so that it transmits light through slits between non-transmitting grooves or ridges.

1 Look at a filament lamp through a coarse grating (1000 lines per cm). (Keep the distance from source to grating large so that nearly plane waves pass through the grating.) What difference do you observe between the zero order maximum and maxima of other orders? Does your observation confirm that different colours of light have different wavelengths? Which colour has the longest wavelength?

2 Now using a fine grating you will concentrate your attention on one maximum (the first order) and on one colour (red). Set up the apparatus as shown in figure 5.27. The grating is placed 1-2 metres from the lamp and held so that its slits are vertical. A red filter is placed in the light path and a metre rule stands on edge, as shown.

3 With one eye closed, move your head so that you can see the first order red maximum. You will also be able to see the ruler. A vertical pointer (a pin held by your partner or by plasticine) can be moved until it coincides with the middle of the red first order maximum. Measure x, the distance of the pointer from the line of the incident wave.

4 Calculate sin θ and so obtain a value for the wavelength of the red light (you will need to know the number of lines per cm).

5 Estimate the percentage error in your value for λ.

6 Observe a point source through two gratings arranged so that their slits are at 90° to each other. What happens to the pattern as one grating is rotated about the direction of the incident light?

7 You can observe similar effects by using the fine mesh of a handkerchief pulled taut, or by observing a distant point source through a stretched umbrella, or by observing a street light through net curtains. Pull the mesh diagonally and record the change you observe.

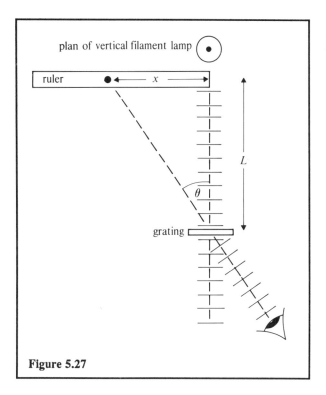

Figure 5.27

EXPERIMENT WV 17

Observing spectra

Apparatus

○ fine diffraction grating (3000 lines per cm)
○ glass prism
○ neon discharge tube (and hydrogen discharge tube,
  if available)
○ e.h.t. supply
○ Bunsen burner
○ red and green filters
○ salt or sodium pencil

1 Connect the e.h.t. supply to a neon discharge tube set
up vertically. Look through the grating at a discharge tube
placed as far away as possible. (The grating lines must be
parallel to the source, e.g. both vertical.) If other discharge tubes are available, observe the spectra of these
sources. How many different wavelengths of light does
the source emit? Give a reason for your answer.

2 Now look at the spectrum emitted by glowing sodium
atoms (figure 5.28). Glowing sodium vapour can be
observed if salt is sprinkled in a Bunsen flame or a piece
of blotting paper soaked in strong brine is wrapped round
the burner and projects a little above the top. Does the
grating separate light from glowing sodium into several
colours? Suggest a reason for your answer.

3 Look at bright white light from a glowing filament lamp
and a fluorescent tube through the grating. Record the
changes you observe when red and green filters are placed
in the beam.

4 Observe the spectrum produced when light from a
distant line filament lamp passes through a prism. Hold
the prism a few centimetres from your eye with the
parallel edges of the prism also parallel to the filament.
Rotate the prism until the spectrum is observed. Which
colour is dispersed most by the prism? What difference
do you observe between the spectrum produced by a prism
and that produced by a grating?

5 (Optional)

You can make a simple spectroscope and look at the Sun's
spectrum using it (figure 5.29).

Note. You must never look directly at the Sun but at a
piece of white paper illuminated by sunlight.

Do you detect any differences between the Sun's spectrum and that of a glowing filament lamp?

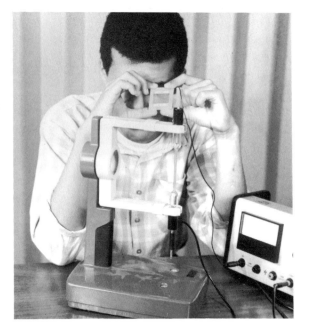

Figure 5.28

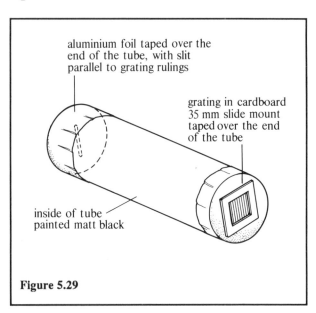

aluminium foil taped over the
end of the tube, with slit
parallel to grating rulings

grating in cardboard
35 mm slide mount
taped over the end
of the tube

inside of tube
painted matt black

Figure 5.29

Questions on objectives

1 Describe, giving the necessary theory, how the wavelength of monochromatic light can be found using Young's slits. Explain briefly how the conditions necessary to produce a stationary interference pattern are satisfied in the experiment. *(objectives 2,3 and 4)*

2 Figure 5.30 shows an arrangement for obtaining Young's fringes. When a monochromatic source of green light is used, the fringe separation is 1.0 mm. Describe briefly what you will see on the screen in the following cases.
(a) The slit separation is reduced to s/2.
(b) The distance D is increased to 3D/2, with the original slit separation.
(c) The slit separation is unchanged, but one slit is made twice as wide as the other.
(d) The original slit arrangement is used, but with a white light source.
(e) With the white light source, a red filter is placed in front of the slits.
(f) With a white light source, the primary slit S is moved slowly in the direction shown by the arrow.
(objectives 4 and 5)

3 Draw a diagram showing the experimental set up for observing single slit diffraction. Show on your diagram the intensity distribution of the light in the plane of observation.
(objective 7)

4 A glass sheet coated with opaque paint has many narrow slits ruled on it at regular spacings to form a grating. It is illuminated by a distant small monochromatic source and a series of bright lines are observed on looking into the grating. What will happen to the position and intensity of these lines if every other slit is blocked out? *(objective 8)*

5 What is a pure spectrum? Outline the requirements for producing a pure spectrum. What are the advantages and disadvantages of a diffraction grating as compared with a prism for studying spectra? *(objective 12)*

6 Explain the term *resolving power of an optical instrument* and state what determines its value. Which has the greater resolving power, the human eye (pupil diameter 2 mm) using light of wavelength 5.0×10^{-7} m or a radio telescope with a dish diameter of 77 m using radio waves of wavelength 21 cm? *(objective 11)*

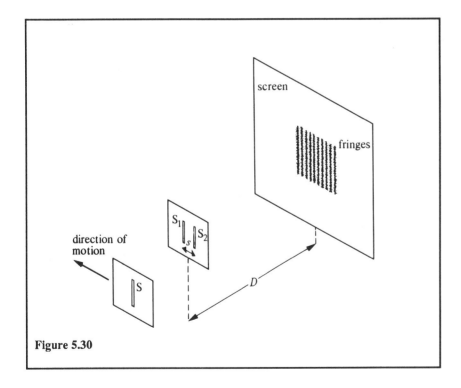

Figure 5.30

Answers

Revision block

R9 (a) 65° (b) 37°

R15 See figure R1. The object is 2cm high, and is 10 cm from the mirror.

R19 (a) See figure R2a. The focal length of the lens is 5.3cm.

(b) See figure R2b. The object is 2.7cm from the lens (half the focal length).

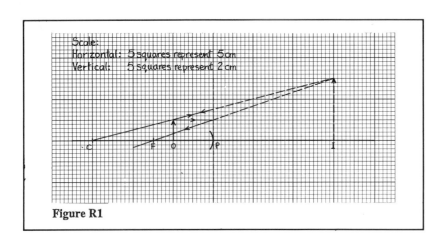

Figure R1

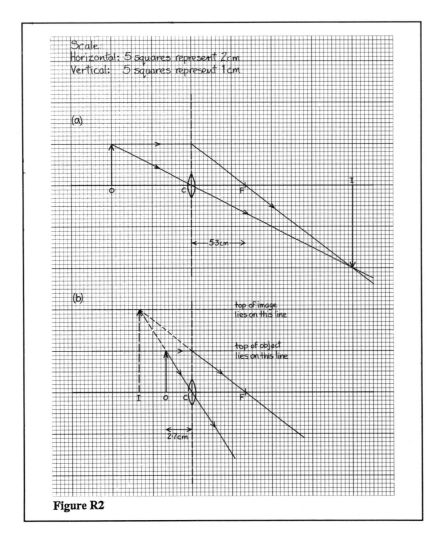

Figure R2

Topic 1

1.1 (a) The water level is forced down by the stone where it hits, but the level around the stone rises.
(b) Intermolecular forces, including surface tension forces.
(c) See figure A1.

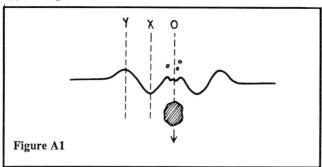

Figure A1

(d) Kinetic energy is transferred to the particles of the water and spreads out through the water as the ripples move.
(e) The moving water particles have inertia. They overshoot the equilibrium position and vibrate, exchanging potential energy and kinetic energy.
1.2 (a) No. The disturbance is not handed on from the source through the medium.
(b) The pulse of starting travels backwards. Its speed depends on the reaction times of the drivers and the distance between cars as they queue.
1.3 (a) To the right.
(b) Yes, to the left.
(c) No. It is only possible to say which way it is moving at instant 7 if we have information about its position at instant 8 as well as instant 6.
1.4 (a) Longitudinal.
(b) Transverse, longitudinal, torsional.
1.5 A displacement-time graph.
1.6 See figure A2.

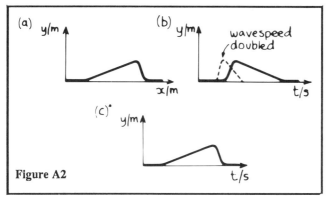

Figure A2

1.7 (a) See figure A3.

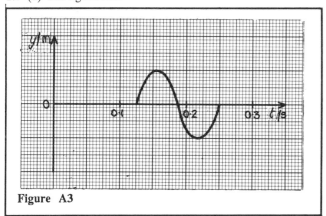

Figure A3

(b) The slope of the tangent to the y against t graph for P is the instantaneous velocity of P.
1.8 (a) See figure A4.

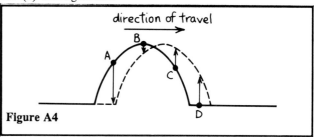

Figure A4

(b) A and B are moving down, C and D are moving up.
(c) A has the greatest average speed. B has the lowest average speed.
(d) At the peak of the pulse.
1.11 (a) Two approaching pulses, superposed at instant 5, mean that the blurred section of the spring is moving up. The pulses are travelling away from each other at instant 7, and must be moving down.
(b) The pulses completely overlap, so that particle displacements are maximum. Particles of the spring move up in the leading half of a pulse and down in the following half. When the pulses overlap the particle velocities are equal and opposite, with a zero resultant.
(c) The amplitude of the pulse is less at the bottom than at the top. Some of the wave energy has been dissipated in heating the spring.
1.12 When the pulse reaches the support, the leading part exerts an upwards force on the support. The support will, therefore, exert a force on the spring in the opposite direction, downwards.
1.13 On striking a rigid support a pulse is inverted—transformed from a crest to a trough, i.e. by half a complete cycle. This corresponds to a π rad phase-change.
At a free end only reversal occurs, crest remaining as crest. There is no phase-change.
1.16 (a) See figure A5.

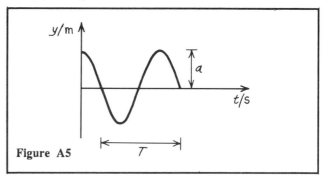

Figure A5

(b) The velocity is given by the gradient of the tangent to the y against t curve.
(c) The gradient and, therefore, the velocity, is maximum when the displacement is zero. The gradient is zero when the particle has maximum displacement.
(d) No. Particles with the same displacement may have identical velocities or equal and opposite velocities.
1.17 (a) (i) A and B, C and D; (ii) A and D, B and C; (iii) A and E.
(b) A and B are moving at the same speed but in opposite directions.
(c) A and E.
(d) One wavelength. As V moves up and down once, a crest at a particular point will be replaced first by a trough and then by the next crest.

(e) 2.4 m s^{-1}. AE is the distance from one crest to the next and is, therefore, one wavelength. The wave travels 1.2 m in 0.5 s.

1.18 (a) Amplitude, frequency (and hence period).

(b) In phase is used to describe vibrations which are in step. Points like A and E have the same displacement and velocity at the same instant, so they are vibrating in phase. As the wave travels along, point B reaches its maximum upward displacement after point A. The vibration of B lags behind the vibration of A, so B has a phase lag behind A.

(c) A and E are consecutive points which are in phase. There will be another point, an equal distance to the right of E, which is also in phase with A and E.

1.19 (a) f is the number of wavelengths passing a fixed point per second, so the distance travelled per second by the waveform = frequency × wavelength.

(b) The wavelength would be increased.

(c) $2 \times 10^5 \text{ Hz}$ (200 kHz)

1.20 See figure A6.

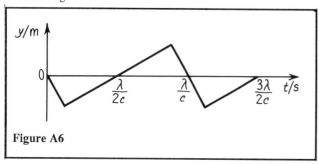

Figure A6

1.21 (a) Spherical.

(b) A circle with source as centre.

(c) Cylindrical with slit as axis.

(d) Circles with slit as centre.

1.22 (a) In the direction opposite to that of the incident pulse.

(b) The pulse is still reflected back in the direction opposite to that of the incident pulse.

1.23 (a) Both pulses are travelling away from the reflector (to the left). The circular wave is travelling directly from the point source. The plane wave pulse is the reflected wave front.

(b) The plane wave contains all the reflected energy, which has been radiated from the source into a larger angle than the direct wave. Also, the smaller amount of energy is distributed over a longer wavefront in the circular wave. Hence, ripples in the circular wave are smaller than those in the plane wave.

(c) Approximately one-third.

1.24 Ripples travel more slowly in shallow water than in deep water. As the ripple is travelling faster towards B and slower towards D, the water depth must increase towards B and decrease towards D. Corner B is tilted down and corner D tilted up.

1.25 The wave energy is concentrated around the headland, producing waves of large amplitude (figure A7). The energy of the wave is less concentrated in the bay, producing waves of smaller amplitude (calmer water).

1.26 The ripples of lower frequency (figure 1.17) have been refracted most.

1.27 (a) The dark circle represent points where two crests meet. The water level is raised by the sum of the amplitudes of the superposed waves.

(b) Half a period later, the dark circle points will be at the bottom of deep troughs.

(c) The water level oscillates between a high crest and a low trough. This is true for each point marked with a dark circle, though the crests and troughs diminish as the wave energy spreads out.

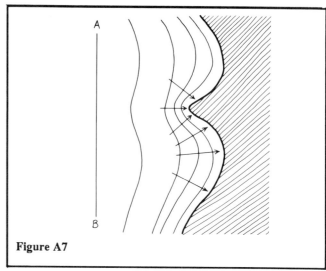

Figure A7

(d) The points marked with blank circles have the same amplitude of vibration as those marked with dark circles. They are, however, out of phase by π rad (opposite phase).

(e) The line of dark and blank circles marks the line along which the surface vibrates with maximum amplitude.

(f) Path difference at P = λ. It is the same for all points along line A_1.

(g) Path difference = $n\lambda$ ($n = 0, 1, 2, \ldots$).

(h) At these points the water will be relatively undisturbed, since a crest and a trough meet at the instant recorded. This will also be true half a period or a whole period later. The vibration at these points has minimum amplitude, and the lines joining these points are nodal lines.

(i) Path difference at $R = 5\lambda/2$, and this is the path difference along line N_3. The path difference along line N_4 is $7\lambda/2$.

1.28 (i) The nodal lines radiate from a point midway between the sources suggesting that $x \approx D$.

(ii) As the source separation d decreases, the separation x of adjacent nodes (calm water) increases. Measurements of photographs 1.19a and 1.19c support the idea that $x \approx 1/d$, because xd is constant.

(iii) Photographs 1.19a and 1.19b show that, for a constant separation of the sources, the distance x between nodes decreases as the wavelength decreases. This suggests that $x \approx \lambda$.

A possible relationship is $x \approx \lambda D/s$.

1.29 (a) 0.75 cm. The wavelength is 3 cm, and for this node the path lengths are 3.75 cm and 5.25 cm, producing a path difference of 1.5 cm (half a wavelength).

(b) Six (see figure A8).

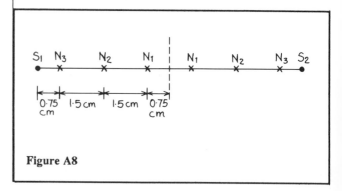

Figure A8

(c) The positions of the nodal points will change, but their separation will still be 1.5 cm. There will now be a node half-way between the sources, and four other nodes along the line between the sources.

(d) There will be no steady interference pattern. There will still be nodes and antinodes, but their positions will change. Every ten seconds the sources will be in step and will produce a pattern like that in part (b). Five second later the pattern will be like that in part (c).

1.31 If the tension is greater, then the force tending to restore the trolley to its equilibrium position will be greater and so will push the pulse along at a faster speed. If the mass is greater, the trolley's inertia will be greater and the pulse will move more slowly.

1.33 (a) The dimensional equation is
$$[L\ T^{-1}] = [M\ L\ T^{-2}]^x \cdot [M\ L^{-1}]^y$$
Equating respective indices on each side,
for [L], $1 = x - y$
for [M], $0 = x + y$
for [T], $-1 = -2x$.
Thus $x = 1/2$ and $y = -1/2$.

(b) The speed of the pulse will increase as it travels down the whip. The mass per unit length μ decreases in the direction in which the pulse is travelling, therefore, since $c \approx 1/\mu^{\frac{1}{2}}$ the speed increases.

1.34 (a) Speed of pulse is 45 m s^{-1}. Time taken is 0.44 s.
$$T = 10\ \text{N}$$
$$\mu = \frac{100 \times 10^{-3}\ \text{kg}}{20\ \text{m}} = 5 \times 10^{-3}\ \text{kg m}^{-1}$$
$$c = \sqrt{\frac{10\ \text{N}}{5 \times 10^{-3}\ \text{kg m}^{-1}}}$$
$$c = 45\ \text{m s}^{-1}$$

(b) Cross-sectional area is 1.1×10^{-6} m^2. Consider a wire of length l and cross-sectional area A.
$$\rho = \frac{m}{V} = \frac{m}{Al}$$
$$\therefore \mu = \rho A$$
$$c = \sqrt{\frac{T}{\mu}} = \sqrt{\frac{T}{\rho A}}$$
$$\therefore A = \frac{T}{c^2 \rho}$$

Topic 2

2.1 (a) 1.7×10^{-2} m (highest frequency), and 17 m (lowest frequency).
(b) 3.3×10^{-6} m

2.2 (a) BD represents particle displacement to the left, AB and DF displacements to the right.
(b) B and F.
(c) O and D.
(d) A, C and E.
(e) See figure A9.

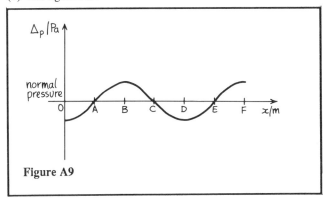

Figure A9

2.3 (i) The personal equation of the observer, that is, the time lag between the observer seeing the flash and operating the timing device.

(ii) The effect of the wind. This can be reduced by taking reciprocal observations (that is, by taking readings for the sound travelling in opposite directions over the same distance at the same time).

(iii) Variable and unknown conditions in the atmosphere over long distances. Temperature and humidity vary locally, and it is not possible to allow for this.

2.4 To produce a distinct image, a surface must treat all parts of the advancing wavefront similarly. It must not introduce a path difference for different parts of the wavefront and must not, therefore, have irregularities greater than a fraction of the wavelength. For sound, with wavelengths of the order of 1 m, the reflecting surface can have irregularities of several centimetres and still produce a distinct sound image. For light, with wavelengths of about 500 nm, the reflecting surface must be highly polished to remove all irregularities greater than a few nanometres.

2.6 (a) The distance between maxima will be increased.
(b) The phase difference is equivalent to introducing a path difference of $\lambda/2$, so the central point of the interference pattern will become a minimum, the positions of the previous minima will become maxima, and so on.

2.8 (a) 252 Hz and 300 Hz.
(b) Adjust the tension of the piano string (to change the frequency of the note) so that the beat frequency decreases. When the string is tuned there will be no beats.

2.10 Observed change in frequency is 250 Hz.
As the source approaches,
$$f_0 = f\left(\frac{c}{c - v_s}\right)$$
$$= f_s\left(\frac{c}{c - c/5}\right)$$
$$= \frac{5}{4} f_s$$
As the source recedes,
$$f_0 = f_s\left(\frac{c}{c + v_s}\right)$$
$$= f_s\left(\frac{c}{c + c/5}\right)$$
$$= \frac{5}{6} f_s$$
Change in frequency $= \left(\frac{5}{4} - \frac{5}{6}\right) f_s$
$$= \frac{5}{12} f_s$$
$$= 250\ \text{Hz}$$

2.11 (a)
$$f_0 = f_s\left(\frac{c}{c - v_s \cos\theta}\right)$$
(b) $f_0 = f_s$
(c)
$$f_0 = f_s\left(\frac{c}{c + v_s \cos\theta}\right)$$

2.12 (a) The observed frequency f_0 is given by
$$f_0 = f_s\left(\frac{c}{c - v_s \cos\theta}\right)$$
therefore
$$f_0 = \left(\frac{500 \times 340}{3340 - 60 \cos\theta}\right)\ \text{Hz}$$
When the train is a distance x from N (figure A10a)

$$\cos \theta = \frac{x}{\sqrt{(50^2 + x^2)}}$$

Substituting for x, and hence θ, gives the following values.

x/m	$60 \cos \theta$/m s^{-1}	f_s/Hz
200	58.2	603
100	53.7	594
50	42.4	571
20	22.3	535
0	0	500

(b) When the train is receding, the following values are obtained.

x/m	f_0/Hz
−20	469
−50	444
−100	432
−200	427

The graph is shown in figure A10b.
(c) The curve is shown by the dotted line in figure A10b.

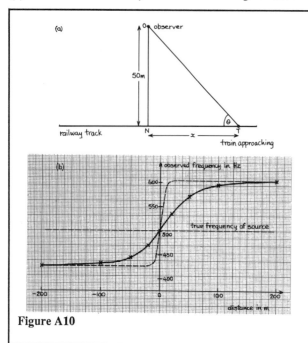

Figure A10

2.14 (a) (i) ∞ (ii) 500 Hz
(b) (i) 2000 Hz (ii) 0
(c) If the source travels at the speed of sound, no sound is heard until the source passes the observer who, at that instant, receives an intense shock wave. After the source has passed, a sound of frequency 500 Hz is heard. An observer approaching the source at the speed of sound hears a sound of twice the emitted frequency. An observer receding from the source at the speed of sound cannot receive any of the emitted sound.
2.15 The beat frequency is 12 Hz. The beats are produced by the superposition of two waves, one from the receding car horn and one reflected from the wall. The reflected wave appears to be coming from an image of the horn, approaching the observer.

For the wave from the receding horn,

$$f_0 = f_s \left(\frac{c}{c + v_s} \right)$$

$$= 400 \times \frac{340}{345} \text{ Hz} = 394 \text{ Hz}$$

For the wave reflected from the wall,

$$f_0 = f_s \left(\frac{c}{c - v_s} \right)$$

$$= 400 \times \frac{340}{335} \text{ Hz} = 406 \text{ Hz}$$

The beat frequency is the difference between these two frequencies.
2.16 (a) As the satellite moves from position 1 to position 2 the beat frequency decreases. When it is overhead, at position 2, the beat frequency is zero. As the satellite moves from position 2 to position 3 the beat frequency increases.
(b) For a source approaching a stationary observer,

$$f_0 = f_s \left(\frac{c}{c - v_s} \right)$$

$$f_0 = \frac{f_s}{(1 - v_s/c)}$$

$$f_0 - f_0(v_s/c) = f_s$$

$$f_0 - f_s = f_0(v_s/c)$$

$$\frac{\Delta f}{f_0} = \frac{v_s}{c}$$

Assuming

$$f_0 \approx f_s$$

$$\frac{\Delta f}{f_s} \approx \frac{v_s}{c}$$

2.18 10 m s^{-1}

$$\text{Frequency of microwaves} = \frac{3 \times 10^8 \text{ m s}^{-1}}{100 \times 10^{-3} \text{ m}}$$

$$= 3 \times 10^9 \text{ Hz}$$

For a moving reflecting surface, if v is the speed of the car,

$$\Delta f = \left(\frac{2v}{c} \right) f_s$$

$$v = \frac{c \, \Delta f}{2f_s}$$

$$= \frac{3 \times 10^8 \times 200}{2 \times 3 \times 10^9}$$

$$= 10 \text{ m s}^{-1}$$

2.19 (f) (i) Points which are 1.0 m, 2.0 m, 3.0 m, and 4.0 m from the point $x = 0$. (ii) Points which are 0.5 m, 1.5 m, 2.5 m, and 3.5 m from the point $x = 0$.
(g) The distance is 1.0 m.
(h) This is half the wavelength of the progressive wave.
2.20 (a) See figure A11.

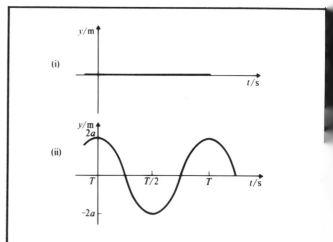

Figure A11

(b) The particles between adjacent nodes appear to move up together and down together (in the case of a transverse stationary wave on a string). They are in phase. The amplitude depends on location between the nodes and varies from zero at a node to a maximum of 2a at an antinode, where a is the amplitude of the progressive waves.

(c) Particles on one side are moving up when particles on the other side are moving down. They are in antiphase—there is a phase difference of π rad.

2.22 The progressive wave takes a time of $T/2$ to travel along the string to the other end, where there is a phase change of π rad, and a time of $T/2$ to travel back to the other end. On reflection, there is a further phase change. At the start of its second run down the string, the reflected wave has taken a time equal to T and has suffered two phase changes and, therefore, it is exactly in phase with the next wave from the source. This reflected wave adds to the next wave; this is repeated in subsequent cycles and a large stationary wave is set up.

2.23 (a) $l = n\lambda/2$ therefore $\lambda = 2l/n$. From $c = f\lambda$, $c = f(2l/n)$ therefore $f = n(c/2l)$.

(b) The phase difference between the incident and reflected waves will be constantly changing and the resulting superposition will, therefore, be changing. The string is being subjected to **forced vibrations**.

(c) (i) The amplitude of the reflected waves is less than that of the incident waves, therefore, they cannot completely cancel each other.

(ii) The system is damped because energy is being transferred from the string to the surroundings. Damping decreases the sharpness of the resonance peaks and, therefore, broadens the frequency response so stationary wave patterns of fairly large amplitude can be obtained at frequencies which are not quite equal to the natural frequency.

2.24 (a) Speed of pulse is 70 m s^{-1}.

Using $c = \sqrt{\dfrac{T}{\mu}}$

$$c = \sqrt{\frac{4.9 \text{ N}}{1.0 \times 10^{-3} \text{ kg m}^{-3}}} = 70 \text{ m s}^{-1}$$

(b) Length of string is 2.1 m.

Using $c = f\lambda$ we have

$$\lambda = \frac{70 \text{ m s}^{-1}}{50 \text{ s}^{-1}} = 1.4 \text{ m}$$

Thus, distance between consecutive nodes is 0.7 m.

2.26 (i) The excess pressure is a maximum (above normal pressure).

(ii) The excess pressure is a maximum (below normal pressure).

Note. When the particle displacement is a maximum the excess pressure above or below atmospheric pressure is zero.

2.27 See figure A12.

2.28 By coupling the vibrating string to a resonator. The air inside a cavity (e.g. a guitar body) and the material of the instrument (the thin wooden body of the guitar) all vibrate producing much greater vibrations in the surrounding air than would be produced by the string alone.

2.30 (a) 1.4×10^3 Hz

(b) 7.0×10^2 Hz

(c) 5.0×10^2 Hz

2.32 (a) The frequency is inversely proportional to the diameter of the wire.

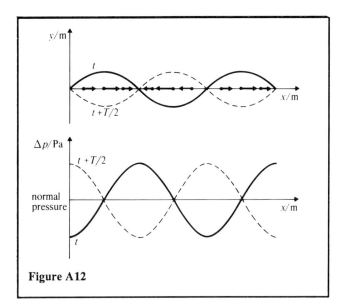

Figure A12

Consider a wire of length l and diameter d,

$$\rho = \frac{m}{v} = \frac{4m}{\pi d^2 l} = \frac{4\mu}{\pi d^2}$$

Hence

$$\mu = \frac{\pi d^2 \rho}{4}$$

$$\therefore f = \frac{1}{l} \sqrt{\frac{T}{\pi d^2 \rho}}$$

(b) 140 N. Substitute values in the equation in (a).

2.33 (a) An alternating transverse force is exerted on the wire, because it is a current-carrying conductor in a magnetic field.

Resonance occurs when the natural frequency of the wire is equal to the main frequency.

(b) 2.5 N

2.34 (a) This is a term which is used to describe the fact that the same note played on different instruments does not sound the same. It depends upon the number of overtones present and their relative intensity.

(b) Fundamental frequency is the lowest frequency obtainable from a string (or pipe).

A harmonic is a note whose frequency is an integral multiple of the fundamental frequency.

An overtone is a note whose frequency is actually obtainable from a string (or pipe).

2.35 f/Hz 256 288 320 341 384 427 480 512

2.36 (a) You can change the length of string with your finger. For violins, shortening the string by about one finger width changes the note by a semitone. Guitars have frets built in to make this easier.

(b) Most stringed instruments have their strings arranged so that their fundamental frequencies are about 5 semitones apart. Thus, a scale can be played by playing 2 or 3 notes on each string before moving to the next.

2.37 (a) (i) The loudness of the note depends upon how hard you blow. (It may be possible to produce a note of higher frequency, i.e. an overtone.)

(ii) Yes. When the length of the air column is increased the frequency of the note decreases.

(b) The pitch of the note changes.

2.41 (a) Length of pipe is 0.52 m.

For a closed pipe, $\lambda/4 = 0.5$ m.

$$f = \frac{340 \text{ m s}^{-1}}{2.0 \text{ m}} = 170 \text{ Hz}$$

The other pipe is longer and, therefore, has a lower frequency. Difference in frequency is 8 Hz.

$$l = \frac{c}{4f} = \frac{340 \text{ m s}^{-1}}{4 \times 162 \text{ s}^{-1}} = 0.52 \text{ m}$$

(b) 425 Hz, 850 Hz, 1275 Hz, 1700 Hz.
For an open pipe, $\lambda/2 = 0.40$ m.

$$f = \frac{340 \text{ m s}^{-1}}{0.8 \text{ m}} = 425 \text{ Hz}$$

In an open pipe, all the harmonics are present.

2.42 (a) A graph of l against $1/f$ gives a straight line (figure A13).

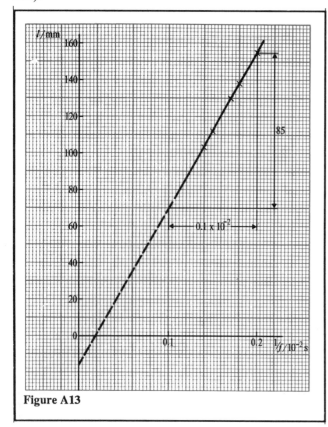

Figure A13

For the first position of resonance, $\lambda/4 = l + x$, where x is the end-correction.
Now $c = f\lambda = 4f(l + x)$
Rearranging, $l = (c/4f) - x$
The gradient of the graph is $c/4$ and the negative intercept on the l-axis is x.
(b) The position of the displacement antinode is a short distance x beyond the end of the tube, where x is the end-correction and equals $0.6 \times$ radius of tube.
From the graph, $x = 16$ mm, so the radius of the tube = 27 mm.
(c) Speed of sound at 273 K is 330 m s^{-1}.

$$\text{Gradient of graph} = \frac{85 \times 10^{-3} \text{ m}}{0.1 \times 10^{-2} \text{ s}} = 85 \text{ m s}^{-1}$$

thus $c = 4 \times 85 \text{ m s}^{-1} = 340 \text{ m s}^{-1}$
Use $c \propto \sqrt{T}$ to correct for temperature.

Topic 3

3.5 The refractive index of a material depends on the frequency (colour) of the light. The speed of blue light in a medium is less than the speed of red light, so blue light is refracted more than red light. Therefore, the refractive index of the medium is greater for blue light than for red light.

3.6 (a) It will be refracted away from the normal, since it is travelling from a dense to a less dense medium.
(b) Angle of refraction in water = 59.5°.
Using $n_1 \sin i_1 = n_2 \sin i_2$, where i_2 is the angle of refraction in water.

Therefore $\quad \sin i_2 = \dfrac{1.50}{1.33} \times \sin 50°$

and $\quad i_2 = 59.5°$

3.8 Refractive index of turpentine = 1.48.

Using $\quad n = \dfrac{\text{real depth}}{\text{apparent depth}}$

$$n = \frac{4.00 \text{ cm}}{2.70 \text{ cm}} = 1.48$$

3.9 (a) The angle of refraction increases.
(b) The maximum value of the angle of refraction is 90°.
3.10 (a) $n_2 \sin c = n_1 \sin 90°$, and since $\sin 90° = 1$,

$$n_1/n_2 = \sin c, \quad \text{or} \quad n_2/n_1 = 1/\sin c$$

(b) $c = 41.8°$.
If $n_a = 1$, $1.50 \times \sin c = 1 \times \sin 90°$.
Therefore, $\sin c = 0.67$, and $c = 41.8°$.
(c) The light must be travelling from a dense to a less dense medium. The angle of incidence in the denser medium must be greater than the critical angle.
(d) The angle of refraction seems to have a sine greater than unity, which is impossible. Mathematical impossibility corresponds to physical non-existence.
3.12 (a) For refraction at P,

$$n_a \sin 90° = n_g \sin c$$

For refraction at Q,

$$n_g \sin (90° - c) = n_a \sin \theta,$$

but $\quad \sin (90° - c) = \cos c,$

so $\quad n_g \cos c = n_a \sin \theta$

Dividing this equation by the first one,

$$\frac{\cos c}{\sin c} = \frac{\sin \theta}{1}$$

so $\quad \sin \theta = \dfrac{1}{\tan c}$

(b) The greatest value that the refractive index may have is 1.41.
The critical angle c has a minimum value when the light leaves AD at grazing emergence ($\theta = 90°$). Then $\tan c = 1$, and $c = 45°$. The maximum value of refractive index is given by $n_g/n_a = 1/\sin 45°$, so $n_g = 1.41$.
(c) The light will emerge from face DC after total internal reflection at face AD. This will occur for all rays for which total internal reflection occurs at face AD.
3.16 (a) $f = +15$ cm, $v = -20$ cm.
(b) $f = -20$ cm, $u = +10$ cm.
3.17 (a) The image is 20 cm from the lens, virtual, erect and twice the size of the object.

Using $\dfrac{1}{f} = \dfrac{1}{u} + \dfrac{1}{v}$

$$\frac{1}{+20 \text{ cm}} = \frac{1}{+10 \text{ cm}} + \frac{1}{v}$$

Using $m = \dfrac{v}{u}$ (numerically), $m = \dfrac{20}{10} = 2$

(b) A diverging lens forms a virtual image of a real object.
(c) The object is 30 cm from the lens and is 6 cm high.
Substituting the values $f = -15$ cm and $v = -10$ cm in the lens formula gives

$$\frac{1}{-15 \text{ cm}} = \frac{1}{u} + \frac{1}{-10 \text{ cm}}, \text{ so } u = +30 \text{ cm}$$

$$m = \frac{10 \text{ cm}}{30 \text{ cm}} = \frac{1}{3}$$

3.18 (a) See figure A14. The parallel beam of light converges towards O_1, the principal focus of the converging lens. O_1 acts as a virtual object for the diverging lens, and the final image is formed at I.

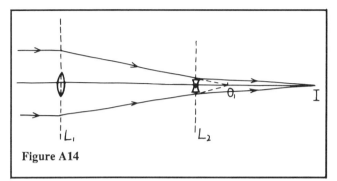

Figure A14

(b) A real image is formed, 6.7 cm from the diverging lens L_2. For L_2, $f = -20$ cm and $u = -(20 - 15)$ cm $= 5$ cm.

Therefore
$$\frac{1}{-20 \text{ cm}} = \frac{1}{-5 \text{ cm}} + \frac{1}{v}$$

$$v = \frac{20}{3} \text{ cm}$$

3.23 (a) The mirror is 9 cm from the object.
Using $m = v/u$, $4 = (45 \text{ cm} - u)/u$, so $u = 9$ cm.
(b) The radius of curvature of the mirror is 24 cm.
Using $1/f = 1/u + 1/v$, where $v = -36$ cm because the image is virtual, $f = 12$ cm so $r = 24$ cm.
(c) The object must be moved 6 cm away from the mirror. The image is now real, therefore $v = +4u_1$, where u_1 is the new object distance.

So $\quad \dfrac{1}{12 \text{ cm}} = \dfrac{1}{u_1} + \dfrac{1}{4u_1}$ and $u_1 = 15$ cm

3.25 The angle which each car subtends at the eye must be the same. The toy car is closer to the observer, and appears to be the same size as the real car which is further away.
3.27 (a) Angular magnification is the ratio of the apparent sizes of the image and the object. Linear magnification is the ratio of the actual sizes.
(b) $M = \beta/\alpha$, where β is the angle subtended at the eye by the final image and α is the angle subtended at the eye by the object at the near point, without the microscope.
3.30 (a) $f = +50$ mm, since $6 = (250 \text{ mm}/f) + 1$.
(b) $u = 300/7$ mm; $M = D/u = 35/6$.
(c) (i) M is maximum for an image at the near point; (ii) M is minimum for an image at infinity.
3.31 (a) A real image of the top of the object, at distance f_0.
(b) A virtual inverted image, at infinity.
(c) A real image, which is erect but is seen by the eye as inverted, because the brain is 'programmed' to deal with inverted images on the retina.
(d) The sum of the focal lengths, $(f_0 + f_e)$.
3.33 (a) Angular magnification = 20.
(b) 25/6 cm (the final image is virtual, so $v = -25$ cm).
(c) 24
3.36 If the exit pupil is larger than the eye pupil, only part of the light passing through the telescope will enter the eye. A smaller objective will serve just as well.
(b) 4.2 cm from the eyepiece.
(c) 48 mm, to give a 2 mm diameter exit pupil.

3.37 The intermediate image must be formed in the focal plane of the eyepiece. In this position, all rays of light which leave the eyepiece are parallel and thus appear to come from infinity. Both the object and image distances increase.
3.40 (a) The image formed by the objective lens is 200 mm from the lens. The linear magnification is 4, so the image is 8.0 mm long.
(b) The final image formed by the eyepiece is 300 mm from the eyepiece. The linear magnification is 6, so the final image is 12.0 mm long.
(c) Using $M = \beta/\alpha$ where $\beta = 12.0/300$ and $\alpha = 2.0/250$ (since the least distance of distinct vision is 250 mm), the angular magnification is 5.

Topic 4

4.2 (Three properties from each group, (a) and (b) below, should be given.)
(a) (i) They transfer energy from place to place.
(ii) They are diffracted.
(iii) They obey the principle of superposition.
(iv) They may undergo a phase change of π on reflection. (Reflection and refraction are *not* possible answers, since they are not exclusive wave properties.)
(b) (i) They are generated by accelerating particles.
(ii) They do not require a material medium.
(iii) They travel at 3×10^8 m s^{-1} in vacuum.
(iv) They are emitted and absorbed by matter, absorption producing an increase in the internal energy of matter.
(v) They show certain properties which require a photon model.
(c) The frequency of the radiation and hence its wavelength in vacuum.
4.4 (a) The field is in the direction X to Y, and is decreasing.
(b) (i) Clockwise, (ii) B perpendicular to E.
4.5 See figure A15.

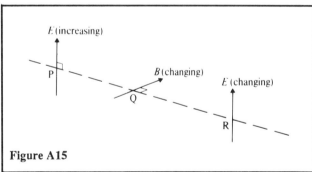

Figure A15

(a) Horizontal.
(b) In a vertical plane containing line PQR.
(c) Vertical.
4.6 The sparks in the spark gap detector are a manifestation of the energy carried from the induction coil transmitter by the electromagnetic waves.
4.7 A quantum of visible radiation is less than the ionisation energy of a gas and so interaction between gas atoms and light does not produce ionisation. X-ray quanta are able to ionise a gas. As a result of this ionisation, X-ray energy is absorbed by a gas but there is no such absorption of light energy. Light waves are, therefore, more penetrating in a gas than X-rays.
4.9 Reflection. Radio waves with wavelengths of the order of several centimetres.
4.10 (a) Microwaves, if they are generated in oscillating circuits, but this frequency range is shared with infra-red radiation and the latter name could also be used.

(b) Absorption by walls, doors, etc. This is a property characteristic of infra-red radiation and very high frequency microwaves which is not possessed by other radio frequencies.

4.11 (a) 50 cm

(b) 50 m

4.12 At 150 km from the receiver, the sky wave and ground wave have similar amplitudes and they will superpose to produce an interference pattern. If the height of the ionosphere varies, the path difference at the receiver will change. This produces a variation in signal strength at the receiver: one moment it is at a maximum of the pattern and the next at a minimum (nearly zero). Variations in the amplitude of the reflected wave (caused by changes in the ionosphere density) will also produce changes in the amplitude at the receiver. At greater distances, only the sky wave will reach the receiver and the interference effect is eliminated.

4.13 (a) Tobacco smoke particles are smaller than the wavelength of light and blue light is scattered more than red light by these particles. The water drops formed at the spout of a kettle are much larger than visible wavelengths and so all visible wavelengths are scattered significantly—hence the 'steam' is white.

(b) Light from the sun has been scattered in the atmosphere. Since short wavelengths are scattered more than long wavelengths, the blue component of the white light predominates in the scattered light so the sky looks blue. Looking at the sun, unscattered light coming from this direction is, therefore, deficient in blue. Higher in the atmosphere there is less scattering; as the astronaut rises, the sky darkens to deep blue and eventually black; and the sun appears progressively whiter.

(c) Infra-red rays are not scattered much by tiny water particles in the mist because of their longer wavelength.

4.14 A wave travelling directly and a wave reflected from an aircraft will be superposed at the aerial. The path difference will determine the strength of the resultant signal and, as the reflector is moving, the aerial will be alternately a point of maximum and minimum signal strength. At maximum a clear picture will be seen; at minimum the picture becomes distorted or disappears.

4.15 Short waves (microwaves) cannot be diffracted around fair-sized obstacles and do not bend round the curved earth. They must be beamed in straight lines from a transmitter to a receiver (in line of sight), which re-transmits the signal to the next microwave receiver/transmitter station.

4.17 See figure A16.

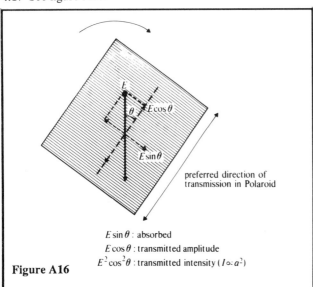

$E \sin \theta$: absorbed
$E \cos \theta$: transmitted amplitude
$E^2 \cos^2 \theta$: transmitted intensity ($I \propto a^2$)

Figure A16

4.18 Polaroid headlamp filters and driving glasses are used with the Polaroid arranged so that both glasses and headlamp filters transmit light whose plane of polarisation is in the same diagonal plane for all cars (e.g. at 45° to the vertical and the horizontal off-side direction). Drawing a sketch will help you to visualise the effect. The driver will see clearly the light of his own headlight beam reflected from the road but the oncoming traffic will produce a plane polarised headlight beam which is crossed with respect to the driver's glasses. The oncoming headlights will be very faint; he will detect the car because of the unpolarised beam from the side lights.

4.20 (a) Light reflected from the ground is partially plane-polarised, and much of this light energy can be absorbed by Polaroid to reduce glare.

(b) Polaroid absorbs most of the nearly plane-polarised light reflected from the water surface, but nearly 50% of the unpolarised light coming up through the surface will pass through the Polaroid (see figure A17) to show the inside of the river.

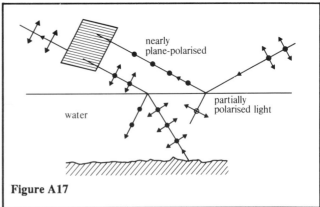

Figure A17

4.21 If light is transverse vibration, then light scattered through 90° at the moon's surface, as a result of reflection and scattering at the surface, will be nearly plane-polarised (see experiment WV10). With the sun on your left or right, look at a patch of sky from which the light to your eye is at right angles to the earth-sun direction. Rotate the Polaroid. If there is extinction in one position the light is plane-polarised.

4.22 The light from a half moon has been turned through 90° at the moon's surface, as a result of reflection and scattering at the surface, and will be nearly plane-polarised.

Topic 5

5.1 (a) They must be the same.

(b) Yes.

(c) They must have the same frequency of vibration and a constant phase relationship.

(d) Yes, they are coherent and would produce a steady pattern.

(e) The flute players would have a different but constant phase relationship, so a new pattern would be set up. The nodes and antinodes would be in different places from those in (c), but with the same separation.

(f) No. Players taking random pauses for breath would produce waves whose frequencies were the same, but the phase relationship would be constantly changing.

5.2 (a) TS_2 represents the path difference at P.

(b) Triangle S_1PT is an isosceles triangle, so the line PM bisecting the base S_1T is also perpendicular to the base.

(c) MP will rotate to the position MO.

(d) Angle θ = angle S_2S_1T.

(e) Angle S_1TS_2 is one of the equal base angles of the isosceles triangle S_1PT. Since angle S_1PT is very small, each base angle is approximately 90°. (Angle S_1PT is less than 0.001 radians (0.06°) for apparatus of the dimensions given.)
(f) Triangles TS_1S_2 and OMP are similar since they have equal angles.
(g) The distance x is very small compared with D, so PM ≈ OM. Therefore, $TS_2/S_1S_2 = OP/OM$, and substituting in this equation gives $p/s = x/D$, or $p = sx/D$.
(h) The approximations can be justified by considering typical experimental values. If $x = 1$ cm and $D = 1$ m, $\theta = 0.01$ radian or 0° 36′. Since OP = MP cos θ, OP = MP × 0.9999 (using 4-figure tables).
5.3 (a) Path differences for the first bright fringe = λ. Therefore $sx_1/D = \lambda$, or $x_1 = \lambda D/s$.
(b) For the second bright fringe, the path difference is 2λ, so $x_2 = 2\lambda D/s$.
(c) $x_n = n\lambda D/s$.
(d) $x_{n+1} = (n + 1)\lambda D/s$.
(e) Separation $= x_{n+1} - x_n = \lambda D/s$.
(f) Fringe separation is independent of n, so the fringes are equidistant and parallel to the original slits.
5.4 The fringe separation x is 7.1×10^{-4} m, so

$$\lambda = \frac{1.0 \times 10^{-3} \text{ m} \times 7.1 \times 10^{-4} \text{ m}}{1.20 \text{ m}}$$

$$= 5.92 \times 10^{-7} \text{ m}$$

5.5 Use the largest convenient value of D (e.g. 40 mm), and measure x for the central fringe. For the direct measurement of λ, find the length of a wavetrain of 8 or 9 ripples.
5.6 (a) Let the fringe spacings for the blue and yellow light be x_b and x_y respectively.

$$x_b = \frac{4.5 \times 10^{-7} \times 2}{5 \times 10^{-4}} = 1.8 \times 10^{-3} \text{ mm}$$

$$x_y = \frac{6.0 \times 10^{-7} \times 2}{5 \times 10^{-4}} = 2.4 \times 10^{-3} \text{ mm}$$

(b) See figure A18a.
(c) See figure A18b. There will be intense blackening, corresponding to a bright fringe, every 7.2 mm.

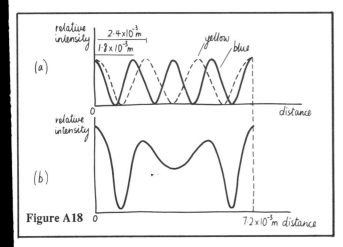

Figure A18

5.7 (a) and (b) See figure A19.
(c) At 0. The path difference is zero here and constructive superposition occurs for all wavelengths.
(d) White central fringe with red edges.
(e) The first order fringe is white with a blue edge near the centre O and a red edge away from O. The central fringe is symmetrical; the other fringes are not. The first order fringes

have lower maximum intensity, and are wider than the central fringe because the patterns due to different colours are becoming more out of step.
(f) There is no region of minimum between the first and second order fringes.
(g) About five fringes can be observed (the central figure plus two on each side) before the various fringe patterns get so much out of step that maxima and minima cannot be observed and uniform whiteness results.
5.8 (a) The pattern will be displaced in the opposite direction (that is, the zero order central fringe will move below O).
(b) The pattern will be displaced along the screen in the same direction (central fringe moving up).
(c) If S moves towards the slits the fringe pattern may appear brighter as more light passes through the slits S_1 and S_2. The pattern could disappear if S is so near that light does not spread out (diffract) enough to pass through the slits.

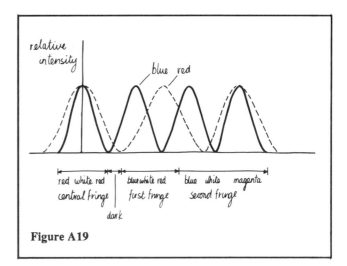

Figure A19

5.10

$$\frac{\lambda_{\text{sound}}}{\lambda_{\text{light}}} = 4 \times 10^6$$

5.11 In figure 5.7a the aperture width is just less than a wavelength and the ripples are diffracted through a wide angle. In figure 5.7b the aperture width is about four wavelengths and most of the wave energy travels forward within a small angle around the original incident direction. A small proportion of wave energy is diffracted into the region of the 'shadow' when compared with figure 5.7a. The pattern in figure 5.7b shows strong waves travelling in certain directions with calmer water between these directions.
In figure 5.7c there is no significant diffraction effect for waves travelling through the central region of the wide aperture. Diffraction effects are limited to the part of the wavefront travelling near to the edge of the aperture.
In figure 5.7d the aperture width is of the order of the wavelength and the diffraction pattern is similar to figure 5.7a. The factor which determines the character of each pattern is the factor wavelength/aperture width, or λ/a. If $\lambda/a \approx 1$, waves are diffracted through large angles. If $\lambda/a \ll 1$, no significant diffraction occurs (except at the edges).
Diffraction of light waves at a slit confirms that narrow slits produce waves diffracted through large angles. Fringes are seen in a single slit diffraction pattern of light waves and figure 5.7b shows similar variations in the intensity of the ripples.
5.12 A line of speakers sending sound through a large slit, e.g. 1 m × 20 cm. Detection could be by microphone and meter or c.r.o.

5.13 (a) Amplitude.

(b) See figure A20. The resulting amplitude can be obtained from a graph (figure A20a) or by using addition of vectors a_1 and a_2 making angle ϕ (phase difference) with each other (figure A20b).

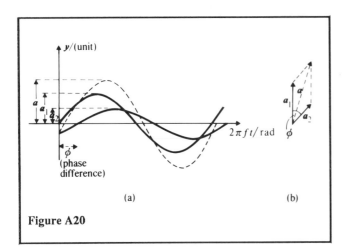

Figure A20

Note. These vectors representing wave amplitude and phase are called phasors and will be used in the unit *Electromagnetism* for a.c. circuits, but a phasor treatment of wave superposition is not required.

(c) Intensity is proportional to (amplitude)^2.

5.14 (a) Yes; see figure A21.

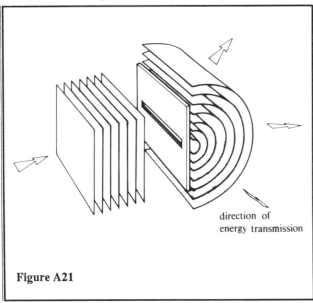

direction of
energy transmission

Figure A21

(b) A plane wavefront would be propagated to the right. A new wavefront is always the envelope of all the separate disturbances produced by point sources on the original wavefront (Huygens' principle).

5.15 (a) $a/2$

(b) $\dfrac{a \sin \theta_1}{2}$

(c), (d) and (e) Darkness.

(f) $\lambda = a \sin \theta_1$, or $\sin \theta_1 = \lambda/a$.

(g) For angles less than θ_1, the path difference between each pair of strips is less than $\lambda/2$ so the waves do not produce a zero resultant.

(h) The effect of the whole wavefront passing through the slit can be found by adding the effects of pairs of slits $a/4$ apart. Resulting effect: minimum light intensity for $\sin \theta_2 = 2\lambda/a$.

(i) If the waves from two narrow strips $a/6$ apart have a path difference $\lambda/2$ at angle θ_3, then

$$\frac{a}{6} \sin \theta_3 = \frac{\lambda}{2},$$

so

$$\sin \theta_3 = \frac{3\lambda}{a}$$

5.16 (a) θ is small; most of the light travels straight ahead (rectilinear propagation).

(b) (i) 0.68 rad or 40°, (ii) π radians or 180°.

(c) (i) The intensity of the image will fall,

(ii) Photographically, by increasing the exposure time.

5.17 See figure A22.

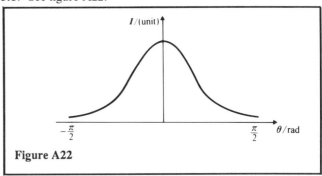

Figure A22

5.18 (a) Figure 5.8e.

(b) Very wide slit or no slit at all (the photograph is of a line source without a diffracting slit).

(c) 2λ. The widths of the central maxima in figures 5.8c and 5.8d are in the ratio $1:2$, so

$$\text{Width of central maximum} = \frac{1}{\text{slit width}}$$

(d) Yes. In figure 5.8, the angular width of the central maximum ($2\lambda/a$) is twice the angular separation of adjacent minima (λ/a). In figure 5.11 the width of the central maximum is twice the distance between minima.

5.19 The diffracted waves probably do not overlap. Suggest making the slit separation smaller. Narrower slits give more spread due to diffraction but, if the slits are too narrow, not enough light will pass through for him to observe the effect. The most appropriate compromise is to have the slits very close together and not too narrow.

5.21 By admitting only the shortest wavelengths of visible radiation the resolving power of the telescope is increased (θ is decreased, since $\theta = \lambda/D$).

5.22 $\sin \theta_1 = \lambda/s$, $\sin \theta_2 = 2\lambda/s$.

5.24 $\sin \theta_1 = \lambda/s$, $\sin \theta_2 = 2\lambda/s$. Draw tangents to the zero, first and second order diffracted waves and measure the angles between these tangents. Measure λ and s on the diagram and write down values of λ/s, $2\lambda/s$, $\sin \theta_1$ and $\sin \theta_2$.

5.25 (a) 4.8×10^{-7} m.

$$\sin 20° = 0.35 = \frac{\lambda}{1.7 \times 10^{-6} \text{ m}}$$

also

$$\sin 45° = \frac{2\lambda}{1.7 \times 10^{-6} \text{ m}}$$

(b) Third order maxima are not visible, since $3\lambda/s = 1.05$ and $\sin \theta_3$ must be $\leqslant 1$.

(c) First minima of slit pattern are at 55°, therefore,

$$\sin 55° = \frac{\lambda}{a}$$

$$a = \frac{4.8 \times 10^{-7} \text{ m}}{0.80}$$

$$= 6.0 \times 10^{-7} \text{ m}$$

5.26 Increasing the angle of incidence reduces the path difference between light reflected from adjacent slits. Since the gramophone record acts as a very course grating only oblique reflection will produce the lower order maxima ($n = 1, 2, 3$, etc.) which are seen as spectra of the fluorescent tube. At smaller angles of incidence higher orders of diffraction maxima are seen, but the overlapping of these orders prevents a clear spectrum being seen. To produce a good spectrum the axis of the tube should be parallel to those grooves which are acting as a grating.

5.27 Angle between second order maxima = 0.01 rad, therefore $\theta_2 = 0.005$ rad $\approx \sin \theta_2$

$$s = \frac{2\lambda}{\sin \theta_2} = \frac{12 \times 10^{-7}}{0.005} \text{ m} = 2.4 \times 10^{-4} \text{ m}$$

Slit (threads) per metre $= 1/s = 4.2 \times 10^3 \text{ m}^{-1}$

5.28

(a)	(b)
1 Narrow slit	to produce a line object
2 Converging lens (collimator)	to produce a parallel beam
3 Prism or grating	to disperse the light into its separate wavelengths
4 Focusing lens or telescope	to project an image on a screen to produce an image in the eye

5.30 The dispersion by a fine grating is greater than that produced by a prism, so more lines are resolved. The grating can be of the reflection type, which is advantageous in avoiding absorption by a prism (or lenses used with a prism) of infrared and ultraviolet.

Index

References

These textbooks may be referred to at the start of each topic. Full details are to be found in the *Student's resource book.*

Avison   Avison, J . *The World of Physics.*
                 Nelson

Duncan   Duncan , T. *GCSE Physics.*
GCSE   John Murray

Duncan   Duncan, T. *Success in Physics.*
SIP   John Murray

Akrill   Akrill, T.B. Bennet, G.A.G. and Millar, C.J. *Physics.*
                 Edward Arnold

Bolton   Bolton, T. *Patterns in Physics.*
                 McGraw-Hill

Duncan   Duncan, T. *Physics: A text book for advanced level students.*
                 John Murray

Muncaster   Muncaster, R. *A-level Physics.*
                 Stanley Thornes

Nelkon   Nelkon, M. and Parker, P. *Advanced Level Physics.*
                 Heinemann

Whelan   Whelan, P.M. and Hodgson, M.J. *Essential Principles of Physics.*
                 John Murray

Acknowledgements

Thanks are due to the following, who have kindly permitted the reproduction of copyright photographs: Page 9, Popperfoto: Figs 1.7, 1.9, 1.14, 1.17, 2.7 EDC Inc,. Mass. USA: Page 27, ARDEA: Figs 3.8, 3.17, Science Photo Library: Page 63 Hungaofilm: Page 77 Prof.Guattori, University of Rome.

The following photographs are by Martin Sookias and Martin Thornton; Figs 1.25, 2.16, 2.18, 3.12, 3.19, 3.20, 4.17 (a) & (b), 5.26.
The following photographs are by Tony Langham; Cover and Figs 1.21, 1.22, 1.23, 2.19, 5.28.

Every effort has been made to contact the copyright holders of Figs, 1.9, 5.3, 4.9, 5.7, 5.8, 5.7, 5.14, 5.15 , 5.16 who kindly gave permission for reproduction in the first edition. The authors and publishers regret these omissions and will be pleased to rectify them in future printings.

Question 9, page 25 Oxford & Cambridge Schools Examination Board, Nuffield O level Physics.